For our very special and beautiful gifts, Tabitha, Jasper and Imani.

Delicious Gifts

Give, Love, Bake

Rob and Amber Kirby

A.

Absolute Press
An imprint of Bloomsbury Publishing
Plc

50 Bedford Square 1385 Broadway
London   New York
WC1B 3DP   NY 10018
UK   USA

www.bloomsbury.com

ABSOLUTE PRESS and the A.
logo are trademarks of Bloomsbury
Publishing Plc

First published in the UK in 2017 by
Absolute Press

© Robert Kirby, 2017
Photography © Jodi Hinds, 2017

Robert Kirby has asserted his right
under the Copyright, Designs and
Patents Act, 1988, to be identified as
Author of this work.

No responsibility for loss caused to any individual or organization acting on
or refraining from action as a result of the material in this publication can be
accepted by Bloomsbury or the author.

British Library Cataloguing-in-Publication Data
A catalogue record for this book is available from the British Library.

Library of Congress Cataloguing-in-Publication data has been applied for.

2 4 6 8 10 9 7 5 3 1

ISBN   HB: 9781472930088
         ePUB: 9781472930095
         ePDF: 9781472930101

Printed and bound in China by C&C Offset

Bloomsbury Publishing Plc makes every effort to ensure that the papers used in
the manufacture of our books are natural, recyclable products made from wood
grown in well-managed forests. Our manufacturing processes conform to the
environmental regulations of the country of origin.

To find out more about our authors and books visit www.bloomsbury.com. Here
you will find extracts, author interviews, details of forthcoming events and the
option to sign up for our newsletters.

Contents

Introduction

Hello and welcome to *Delicious Gifts*. This book was a natural follow on from my previous books, *Cook with Kids* and *The Family Kitchen* which included a chapter called 'The Gift Shop'. This chapter was very popular and generated the most interest and created the biggest buzz from the press and general public alike.

My wife Amber and I have made many bespoke foody presents for family and friends over the years, so this seemed an obvious thing to share. I have cooked for over 30 years and hope you enjoy these tried and trusted recipes.

Amber and I both styled, designed and wrapped each recipe with some fun and quirky twists. We also scoured the world for props and original labels, jars, tins, boxes and bags, searching websites from Europe, Asia and America which was lots of fun and gave each gift bespoke identity.

We hope this book inspires you to take some time out of the fast-paced, time-shy lifestyle we all seem to be leading these days. Show someone you really care by investing a little of your time, energy and creativity in hand-making the perfect and authentic delicious gift.

Enjoy, good luck, but most of all, have fun and let those creative juices flow!

Love Rob

Chapter One:
Cookie Love

Here are eight of our favourite, crunchy, chewy, soft and sweet biscuits. Everybody loves biscuits, making them the perfect gift for any celebration.

The Slice and Bake Sweet and Savoury Biscuit Tubes can be made ahead and stored in the freezer, ready to grab, slice and bake when you have guests and want to impress. Have lots of fun and giggles making the Family Funny Face Cookies to give to your loved ones – and hope they still talk to you afterwards! Last but not least, it's not an official biscuit but the very retro Coconut Macaroon had to sneak into this scrummy, yummy chapter.

Package your bakes in pots, jars, boxes or bags. All these biscuits will keep well for a week stored in a tight sealed container – if they last that long!

Slice and Bake Sweet and Savoury Biscuit Tubes

These will go down a storm with your friends! And the best bit is you can freeze ahead if you feel like getting your bake on one day and making a few batches so you can always have ready supplies.

EACH TUBE MAKES 25 BISCUITS

FOR THE HONEY PECAN BISCUIT TUBES
225g unsalted butter
75g caster sugar
1 egg yolk
1 tablespoon clear honey
250g plain flour, sifted
75g broken pecans

FOR THE SAVOURY CHEESY TUBES
100g Gruyère cheese, grated
100g Parmesan cheese, grated
200g butter
300g plain flour, sifted
½ teaspoon cayenne pepper
  for a fuller flavour (for a milder
  warmth, use ¼ teaspoon)
½ teaspoon English mustard
  powder
50g sesame seeds

To make the honey pecan biscuit tubes, cream the butter and sugar together in a bowl, then add the egg yolk, honey and flour to form a dough. Finally, add the pecan nuts and stir to make sure they are evenly distributed.

Flour a work surface and roll the dough into a tube measuring roughly 5cm in diameter and 25cm in length. Wrap and roll this in baking parchment, or in muslin cloth, twisting the ends so that it looks like a cracker.

Tie the 'cracker' with string and label with the following instructions: Slice with a hot knife into 5mm-thick circles, place on a baking tray and bake in a preheated oven at 180°C/160°C Fan/Gas Mark 4 for 10 minutes until golden brown.

Next, to make the savoury cheesy tubes, cream both cheeses and butter together in a bowl. Fold in the flour, cayenne pepper and mustard powder, then mix to form a firm dough.

Flour a work surface and roll the dough into a tube measuring roughly 5cm in diameter and 25cm in length, then roll in the sesame seeds. Wrap and roll this in baking parchment, or in muslin cloth, twisting the ends so that it looks like a cracker.

Tie the 'cracker' with string and label with the following instructions: Slice with a hot knife into 5mm-thick circles, place on a baking tray and bake in a preheated oven at 180°C/160°C Fan/Gas Mark 4 for 10 minutes until golden brown.

Peanut Butter and Cocoa No-bake Cookies

Deliciously oaty and chocolatey, and a great recipe for the kids to get involved in (or if the oven has blown up!).

MAKES 16

375g caster sugar
4 tablespoons cocoa powder
125ml milk
1 teaspoon vanilla extract
115g butter
120g peanut butter
310g oats

Line a tray with greaseproof paper.

Add sugar, cocoa, milk, vanilla extract and butter to a medium-sized pan. Slowly stir the ingredients together over a gentle heat until the butter has melted, then boil for exactly 1 minute.

Remove the pan from the heat and stir the peanut butter through, then fold in the oats. While the mixture is still warm, use a tablespoon to place mounds of the mixture on the lined tray, then flatten with the back of the spoon.

Place in the fridge or in a cool place to set.

All-in-the-jar Cookie Mix

Easy peasy! You just need to get a 1 litre preserving jar and layer all the ingredients inside.
Attach a label with the baking instructions, et voila!

MAKES 16–18

180g plain flour
½ teaspoon baking powder
100g light brown sugar, sieved
50g caster sugar
100g dried cranberries
100g white chocolate chips
100g dark chocolate chips

TO BAKE THE COOKIES (WRITE THIS
ON THE POSTCARD)
125g butter
1 large egg

Sift the flour and baking powder into a bowl, mix together and spoon into a 1 litre jar. Top with the light brown sugar and then with separate layers of the caster sugar, cranberries, white chocolate chips and, finally, dark chocolate chips.

ON A POSTCARD WRITE:
Empty me into a large bowl, add 125g melted butter and 1 large egg. Stir together to make a firm paste and divide into 16–18 pieces, rolling each one into golf balls. Flatten each one and rest in the fridge for 1–2 hours on a tray lined with greaseproof or silicone paper. Bake me for 12–15 minutes at 180°C/160°C Fan/Gas Mark 4.

Tie the postcard or label around the jar.

Salted Caramel and Popcorn Cookies

The best of both worlds – popcorn and cookies! Bring to friends, kick back, relax and get ready for movie night.

MAKES 12–16

230g soft light brown sugar
115g caster sugar
170g unsalted butter, softened
2 drops of vanilla extract
1 egg
1 egg yolk
450g plain flour, sifted
½ teaspoon baking powder
pinch of salt
icing sugar, for dusting

FOR THE POPCORN
1 teaspoon vegetable oil
100g popcorn kernels

FOR THE CARAMEL
120g soft light brown sugar
120g unsalted butter
100ml double cream
1 teaspoon sea salt

Combine the soft light brown sugar, caster sugar, butter and vanilla extract in a large bowl until you have a smooth creamy mixture. Gradually add and beat in the egg and extra yolk, making sure you mix them in thoroughly. Fold in the sifted flour, baking powder and salt, combining everything to make a dough.

Roll the dough into a sausage shape (about 7cm across). Place on greaseproof paper and chill in the fridge for 2 hours.

Preheat the oven to 180°C/160°C Fan/Gas Mark 4. Line a baking tray with silicone paper.

Once the dough is really firm, slice it into 1.5cm-thick rounds using a warm serrated knife, placing the cookies on the lined baking tray as you go. Bake in the oven for 12–15 minutes. Cool on a wire rack.

Slowly heat the vegetable oil in a deep saucepan over a low heat and add the popcorn kernels. Put a lid on the pan and listen for pops!

To make the caramel, melt the soft light brown sugar and butter together in a saucepan over a low heat. When the mixture turns golden brown, take it off the heat and very carefully whisk in the cream. Stir in the salt and allow the mixture to cool.

Once cool, dust the cookies with icing sugar, then spoon the cooled caramel over and polka dot with popcorn.

Family Funny Face Cookies

Spread a little joy and laughter and give your nearest and dearest the mirror image of themselves in cookie form! Use your local sweet shop for inspirational facial features!

MAKES 6–8 LARGE FACES

FOR THE COOKIES
225g unsalted butter
225g caster sugar
1 egg, beaten
½ teaspoon vanilla extract
pinch of salt
450g plain flour, sifted

FOR THE ICING
1 egg white
250g icing sugar, sifted

FOR DECORATING
sweet selection (strawberry laces,
    Liquorice Allsorts and Smarties)

Line a baking tray with silicone paper.

Cream together the butter and sugar, then add the egg, vanilla extract and salt. Gradually fold in the sifted flour to form a dough.

Roll out the dough on a floured work surface until 5mm thick. Take a large, round, plain cookie cutter (12–14cm in diameter; alternatively cut around a small plate) and cut out the cookie faces. Place on the lined baking tray and rest in the fridge for 1–2 hours.

Preheat the oven to 180°C/160°C Fan/Gas Mark 4. Bake in the preheated oven for 12–15 minutes until golden brown. Cool on a wire rack.

To make the icing, whisk the egg white to a soft foam, then slowly whisk in the icing sugar until the mix is the right texture for piping. Place the icing into a piping bag fitted with a small plain nozzle, then decorate the cooled cookies with icing and sweets, turning your family and friends into cookies!

Polka Dot Jam Jar Cookies

A really cute packaging idea for these is to glue some Smarties to the lid of a glass jar, then spray with varnish and allow to dry. Stack your cookies inside to the brim and give with love.

MAKES 16–20

230g light muscovado sugar
115g caster sugar
170g unsalted butter, softened
2 drops of vanilla extract
1 egg
1 egg yolk
450g plain flour, sifted
½ teaspoon baking powder
small pinch of salt
2½ tubes of Smarties

Combine the muscovado sugar, caster sugar, butter and vanilla extract in a large bowl until you have a smooth creamy mixture. Gradually add and beat in the egg and extra yolk, making sure you mix them in thoroughly. Fold in the flour, baking powder, salt and 2 tubes of Smarties, combining everything to make a dough. Do this carefully as you want to keep the Smarties whole.

Roll this mix into a sausage (about 5cm in diameter). Place onto greaseproof paper and chill in the fridge for 2 hours.

Preheat the oven to 180°C/160°C Fan/Gas Mark 4. Line a baking tray with silicone paper.

Once the dough is really firm, slice it into 1.5cm-thick rounds using a warm serrated knife, placing the cookies on the lined baking tray as you go.

Bake in the preheated oven for 15 minutes, then take the cookies out and while still warm quickly press some extra Smarties into the top. Cool on a wire rack.

Caramelised Big Boaster Stacks

For your nut-loving friends, and perfect paired with a steaming hot espresso. Put in a beautiful jar or pile into an antique-style biscuit tin.

MAKES 20

225g unsalted butter
225g caster sugar
1 egg, beaten
50g hazelnuts, roughly chopped
400g plain flour, sifted

FOR THE CARAMEL
50g butter
200g caster sugar
5 tablespoons water
100g whole hazelnuts
rock salt, for sprinkling

Line a baking tray with silicone paper.

Cream together the butter and sugar in a bowl, then add the egg and chopped hazelnuts. Gradually fold in the sifted flour to form a dough. Roll into 20 golf-ball shapes (each about 50g) and place on the lined baking tray, allowing enough room for them to spread when cooking. Using the palm of a floured hand, gently flatten each to create a cookie shape. Place in the fridge to rest for 1–2 hours.

Preheat the oven to 180°C/160°C Fan/Gas Mark 4. Bake the cookies in the preheated oven for 12–15 minutes until golden brown, remove and leave to cool on a wire rack.

To make the caramel, melt the butter, sugar and water in a heavy-based saucepan over a medium heat and shake gently until the mixture begins to bubble and caramelise to a golden brown. Remove from the heat and carefully pour the whole hazelnuts into the hot caramel – this mix is extremely hot so work carefully.

Shake the pan to mix thoroughly. Quickly take a teaspoon and place 4–5 hazelnuts on each cookie, using another spoon to push the sticky caramelised hazelnuts off the first spoon (they will be too hot to do this with your hands). Work quickly as the caramel sets; if it does, gently re-heat.

Sprinkle with rock salt and serve.

Coconut Macaroons

A nod to the '70s, we've gone a little retro here but some things are worth bringing back. Get creative on the packaging front and use some old coconut shells to hold them.

MAKES 6

110g desiccated coconut
75g caster sugar
1 egg white
6 glacé cherries

Preheat the oven to 170°C/150°C Fan/Gas Mark 3. Line a baking tray with silicone paper.

Combine the coconut and caster sugar in a large bowl. In another bowl, whisk the egg white until it doubles in size and forms stiff peaks. Add in the coconut and sugar mixture and gently fold.

Roll the mixture into 6 golf-ball-sized shapes, placing them on the lined tray as you do so. Flatten them slightly, then pop a cherry into the middle of each macaroon. Bake in the preheated oven for 6–8 minutes, until they are a light golden colour. Cool on a wire rack.

Chapter Two:
For the Pantry

Welcome into the store-cupboard and larder section of the book.

For something a little different, why not try the Pancetta Salt, the perfect seasoning for boiled runny eggs or grilled tomatoes. We glued Percy the Pig on the lid of the jar for a fun and novel packaging idea! The Asian Pickled Watermelon is a triumph and cuts through slow-cooked pork belly perfectly. Lastly, give the Home-made Butter and a jar of the Strawberry, Thyme, Prosecco and Vanilla Jam as a perfectly partnered duo and write on the label 'Show me the hot toast'!

Keep these recipes in a dark, cool pantry or refrigerator. Have fun wrapping, jarring and bottling in this perfect preserving chapter.

Pancetta Salt Jars

This makes a great gift as it's a lovely store-cupboard ingredient. Perfect for sprinkling on Brussels sprouts, creamy pasta sauces and anything you want to add a little smokey, salty hit to.

MAKES 2 JARS

150g pancetta, sliced
250g sea salt flakes
1 teaspoon thyme leaves

Preheat the oven to 200°C/180°C Fan/Gas Mark 6. Line a baking tray with silicone paper.

Place the pancetta on the lined baking tray and cook in the preheated oven for 10–15 minutes until really crispy and dark brown. Place on kitchen paper to cool.

Place the pancetta and sea salt in a food processor and blitz for 3–5 minutes until finely ground. Pour into a bowl, mix in the thyme leaves, then spoon into sterilised jam jars, seal and label. Store in a cool, dark place and use within 2 weeks.

Caramelised Onion, Fig and Toffee Date Chutney

The perfect partner to a decent cheeseboard – it is especially delicious with goat's cheese. You really get the fresh thyme flavour coming through and this will be the point of difference to shop-bought chutneys. We often give jars of this at Christmas and we've lost count of how many times people ask us to make it again.

MAKES 4 SMALL JARS

2 tablespoons vegetable oil
1kg onions, sliced
4 fresh figs, stemmed and diced
10 Medjool dates, halved, stoned and quartered
2 sprigs of thyme
3 bay leaves
75g dark brown sugar
1 teaspoon chopped thyme leaves
100ml balsamic vinegar
sea salt and freshly ground black pepper

Heat the oil in a large saucepan over a medium heat, add the onions, figs, dates, thyme sprigs and bay leaves and cook for around 30 minutes without colouring, stirring occasionally, until soft and tender. Discard the thyme sprigs and bay leaves.

Stir in the sugar, chopped thyme and balsamic vinegar. Reduce the heat and very slowly dry out and caramelise the mixture for around 50 minutes. Make sure the chutney doesn't catch on the bottom of the pan. Season to taste.

Place the hot mixture into sterilised jam jars, seal and allow to cool before storing or serving. Store in the fridge and use within 4 weeks.

Asian Pickled Watermelon

Wowzers, just delish – this starts a party in your mouth! This is absolutely perfect with pork or anything you want to add a little razzmatazz to.

MAKES 1 LARGE JAR

1 watermelon
300ml rice vinegar
200ml water
3 shallots, peeled and thinly sliced
75g fresh ginger, peeled and
   thinly sliced
2 bird's eye Thai chillies, finely
   chopped
150g soft brown sugar
zest and juice of 2 limes
1 lemongrass stick, bashed

Peel the watermelon using a very sharp knife or swivel peeler. It is important to remove only the outer green skin, leaving the white rind on the watermelon. Cut the peeled watermelon into quarters. Using a sharp knife, remove the inner red flesh (and enjoy eating it!), leaving the white rind with just a small amount of red flesh (around 2cm) attached. Cut the rind into 3–4cm cubes and place in a large bowl.

To make the pickling vinegar, add the remaining ingredients to a heavy-based pan and gently bring to the boil, then turn down the heat and leave to simmer for 10 minutes, ensuring the sugar has dissolved.

Remove from the heat, allow to cool slightly, then add to the bowl containing the cubed rind and stir gently. Spoon the watermelon rind and the pickling vinegar into a large sterilised preserving jar, ensuring the watermelon cubes are covered.

Seal while still slightly warm and label. Store in a cool, dark place and eat within 2 weeks.

Pickled Heritage Rainbow Beetroot

Uber cute and a real visual treat. This beautiful beetroot is just crying out for some soft goat's cheese to enjoy alongside.

FILLS A 2 LITRE JAR

1kg small heritage beetroot of
   different colours
500g caster sugar
750ml white wine vinegar
500ml water
6 bay leaves
10 cloves
5 star anise
5 sprigs of fresh thyme

Trim and peel the beetroot, then thinly slice using either a very sharp knife or a mandolin to make thin crisps. Pack the sliced beetroot into a sterilised 2 litre pickling jar. Try to be creative with your colour combinations as you layer in the slices.

Place the caster sugar, white wine vinegar and water in a heavy-based saucepan. Add the bay leaves, cloves, star anise and thyme, then bring to a rapid boil, until the sugar has melted.

Pour the boiling hot mixture over the beetroot, making sure to include all the spices. Seal the jar immediately, then allow to cool.

Store in a cool, dark place until opened, then store in the fridge. Use within 4 weeks of making.

Strawberry, Thyme, Prosecco and Vanilla Jam

This is no ordinary strawberry jam, this is pimped-up strawberry jam! An absolute treat served with Devonshire scones and lashings of clotted cream.

MAKES 3–4 JARS

800g strawberries, hulled and
    quartered
1kg jam sugar
2 vanilla pods, split and seeds
    removed
100ml prosecco
½ teaspoon thyme leaves

Place the strawberries, sugar, vanilla pods and seeds in a large, heavy-based pan and stir well. Heat over medium to high heat, stirring occasionally, then just before the mixture starts to boil and the sugar has all dissolved, add the prosecco and bring to the boil. Continue to boil rapidly and stir for 10–15 minutes, then remove any scum with a spoon.

To test if the jam is ready, spoon a drop onto a chilled saucer – it should form a slight ripple if you drag the spoon through it. If not, boil for an additional 5 minutes and test again.

Discard the vanilla pods and add the thyme leaves. While still hot, pour into sterilised jars, seal tightly and label.

Boozy Buttery Apple Sauce

The possibilities are endless with this! Great with salty pork crackling sticks, spooned into a pie, added to sausagemeat for the tastiest sausage rolls – we could go on but you get the picture!

MAKES 3 JARS

50g caster sugar
2 tablespoons organic honey
50g butter
50ml brandy
1.5kg apples (any variety),
   peeled, cored and sliced
2 teaspoons vanilla extract
1 teaspoon ground cinnamon
30g dark brown sugar

Preheat the oven to 150°C/130°C Fan/Gas Mark 2.

In a small saucepan, combine the caster sugar and honey. Cook over a low heat, stirring occasionally, until the caramel mixture becomes a dark amber colour.

Remove the pan from the heat and carefully add the butter (it will bubble up). Whisk until smooth, then add the brandy, returning to the heat if necessary to ensure it is fully combined.

Combine the apples, vanilla, cinnamon and dark brown sugar in a small roasting tin. Pour the caramel in and toss to coat. Cook in the preheated oven, stirring occasionally, for 2 hours or until dark brown and the apples are mushy.

Use a blender to purée the mixture or pass it through a fine sieve until smooth. Spoon into sterilised jars and store in the fridge. Return to the heat if necessary to soften before serving. Use within 2 weeks.

Hand-tied Homemade Butter

You will not believe how easy it is to make your own butter. Wait until you taste it too
– nothing beats it. You can get really creative with your flavoured butters – add a little
English mustard and finely chopped lovage leaves (perfect with Jersey Royal potatoes) or
replace the sea salt with smoked sea salt, just beautiful!

SERVES 4

600ml double cream
½ teaspoon sea salt

Pour the cream into the bowl of an electric mixer. Using the paddle or whisk, start to beat on a medium setting. After about 6 minutes the cream will look as though it is separating and will take on a yellowy, cottage-cheese appearance.

Continue beating and you will see a liquid coming out – this is the buttermilk. Pour this off into a separate container (use it in other recipes, such as buttermilk chicken), continue beating and keep removing the buttermilk at intervals until a butter-like consistency is achieved and no more liquid appears. This should take around 20–30 minutes.

Finally, fold the salt into the butter. Wrap the butter in baking parchment and tie the ends, then store in the fridge. Use within 2 weeks.

Hazelnut Spread Jars

Heavens above, this is good! In fact, it's finger-licking good. Once that jar's cracked open, you'll be addicted at first taste. It's almost too good to share really.

MAKES 4 JARS

200g dark chocolate, chopped
300ml plus 2 tablespoons
   condensed milk
6 tablespoons clear organic
   honey
200g whole hazelnuts
5 tablespoons warm water
1 tablespoon rock salt
sea salt and hazelnuts, for
   garnishing

Preheat the oven to 190°C/170°C Fan/Gas Mark 5.

Melt the chocolate, 300ml of the condensed milk and honey together in a bowl placed over a saucepan of boiling water, stirring gently.

While the chocolate is melting, roast the hazelnuts on a baking tray in the preheated oven for 8–10 minutes, then place in a food processor. Blitz for 2 minutes, add the remaining 2 tablespoons condensed milk, the warm water and rock salt, then scrape down the sides of the mixing bowl. Continue to blitz for a further 2–3 minutes until smooth and wet.

Add the warm chocolate mixture to the food processor and mix with the hazelnuts for a further 2 minutes until smooth and spreadable in texture. Be careful not to over-mix.

Spoon into sterilised jars and garnish with sea salt and hazelnuts. Store in a cupboard (not the fridge) and use within 2 weeks.

Chapter Three:
At the Deli

The Deli is gift inspired and whenever we travel the world we have fun hunting down the best delis, whether in NYC, Paris or Italy. Here are some of our favourites from around the globe. Hope you love this chapter as much as we do!

We had lots of fun designing and wrapping this selection of goodies. From tins for the Parma Ham and Mozzarella Pizza, to wooden boards for the Orange, Whiskey and Dill Gravadlax and lots of smiles making the Flowerpot Apple and Hazelnut Crumbles with a look straight from the garden shed. The Tasty Tomato and Tarragon Passata and the Chunky Bean and Pea Pesto, styled with its own personal metal dog tag, would proudly grace the finest delis in Italy.

These scrummy fresh gifts won't keep long and need to be eaten on the day of making.

Sea Salt and Thyme Crackling

Get your snout around these! Be warned – they are very, very moreish. Goes perfectly with the Buttery Apple Sauce on page 36 too.

MAKES 10–12 STICKS

300g pork skin (the rind from the
    loin, around 30cm in length and
    16cm wide)
½ teaspoon table salt
1 teaspoon sea salt
1 teaspoon chopped fresh thyme

Trim the pork skin so you have a thin, even covering of around 1cm of fat on the underside.

Season the fat side (non-skin side) of the rind with the table salt. Roll the rind up from one of the short sides, then wrap in clingfilm as tightly as possible and tie both ends to prevent it from unrolling. Place in the freezer for 2 hours. The rind should be frozen but not solid – if it is, leave it to defrost just enough so that you can cut through it.

Preheat the oven to 190ºC/170ºC Fan/Gas Mark 5. Line a baking tray with baking parchment.

Mix the sea salt and thyme together.

Using a sharp serrated knife, cut the frozen rind into slices 5mm thick. Carefully unroll each one and place skin side up on the lined baking tray, leaving a 1cm gap between each slice. Season with the sea salt and thyme and place a second sheet of baking parchment on top, followed by a second baking tray. You will then need to place something heavy and ovenproof on top of the upper baking tray to hold it down (I use a cast-iron casserole dish).

Place in the preheated oven and cook for 30 minutes, checking occasionally. The crackling is ready when golden brown. Remove from the oven, leave to cool for 5 minutes, then drain on kitchen paper. As the sticks of crackling cool they will crisp up more, but they can be eaten warm or cold. Eat within 2 days.

Date, Apricot and Hazelnut Biscotti

These are crying out to be dunked into a steaming hot espresso. A beautiful way to give this would be wrapped in paper and tied with string and a sliced biscotti label.

MAKES 20–26

3 eggs
150g caster sugar
250g plain flour
¼ teaspoon bicarbonate of soda
½ teaspoon baking powder
pinch of salt
75g hazelnuts, roughly chopped
50g Medjool dates, stoned and
  chopped
50g dried apricots, chopped

Whisk 2 of the eggs and the sugar in a bowl until light and fluffy. Sift the flour, bicarbonate of soda, baking powder and salt together in another bowl. Mix this dry combination into the whisked eggs along with the hazelnuts, dates and apricots, mixing together thoroughly. Leave the dough to rest in the fridge for about 1 hour (it should be a bit soft and sticky at this stage).

Preheat the oven to 200°C/180°C Fan/Gas Mark 6. Line a large baking tray with baking parchment.

Once the dough has rested, turn it out onto a floured work surface and roll into a rectangle about 28cm long and 5cm wide. Place this on the lined baking tray. Beat the remaining egg and use to brush the dough.

Bake in the preheated oven for 20 minutes, then check by inserting a skewer – if it comes out clean, it's cooked; if not, bake for another couple of minutes. Leave to cool on the baking tray. Reduce the oven temperature to 170°C/150°C Fan/Gas Mark 3½.

WHEN COOL, PACKAGE AND GIFT WITH THE FOLLOWING INSTRUCTIONS:
Cut into slices 1cm thick and lay flat on a baking tray lined with baking parchment. Bake for 15–20 minutes until golden brown, turning halfway through. Once baked, leave to cool on a wire rack and then store in an airtight container.

Marmite and Double Cheese Twists

You either love it or hate it! We are Marmite lovers in our house and the addition of it gives a delicious savoury note to these twists. Served in a vintage style tin to impress, they are perfect with pre-dinner drinks.

MAKES 20

250g puff pastry
1 tablespoon Marmite
1 tablespoon water
40g Gruyère cheese, finely grated
40g Parmesan cheese, finely grated
1 teaspoon smoked paprika

Preheat the oven to 180°C/160°C Fan/Gas Mark 4. Line a baking tray with greaseproof paper.

Roll out the puff pastry on a floured work surface until about 25cm long, 20cm wide and 5mm thick. Using a sharp knife, cut into about 20 strips, each 1cm wide.

In a small pan, gently warm the Marmite and water until melted and fully incorporated. Allow to cool slightly, then generously brush over the pastry, making sure you go right to the edges. Sprinkle over both cheeses, saving 10g of each for later.

Dust with smoked paprika, then hold each end of a strip and twist to form a spiral shape. Place the spirals on the lined baking tray (push down each end to stop them unravelling) and bake in the preheated oven for 12–15 minutes until golden brown.

Place on a wire rack and scatter over the remaining cheese. Allow to cool.

Tasty Tomato and Tarragon Passata

In the summer our greenhouse is bursting at the seams with tomatoes of all varieties as we have a bit of a fetish for everything with tomatoes. Even our candles are tomato-leaf scent!

MAKES 560ML

1kg ripe tomatoes, chopped
10 garlic cloves, roughly chopped
5 shallots, peeled and chopped
1 x 400g tin of chopped tomatoes
1 bunch of tarragon, roughly chopped
1 tablespoon caster sugar
salt and freshly ground black pepper

Preheat the oven to 160°C/140°C Fan/Gas Mark 3.

Place all the ingredients in a casserole pan and mix together. Cover with silicone paper and roast in the preheated oven for 1½ hours until the mixture has a pulpy texture.

Cool slightly, then push the mixture through a sieve into a bowl, making sure you squeeze all the liquid and pulp through (this will take a lot of determination and muscle, but it is worth it!). Whisk the sieved mixture, season and pour into sterilised jars. Store in the fridge and use within 7 days.

Chunky Bean and Pea Pesto

This is Amber's absolute favourite recipe in this book. It is just summer in a jar! We spread this atop toasted sourdough bread and thickly spread ricotta cheese with maybe a little grated frozen chilli – perfect for a light summer brunch.

MAKES 500G

50g pine nuts
75g fresh or frozen peas, chopped
75g broad beans
1 large bunch of super-fresh basil
50g Parmesan cheese, grated
250ml olive oil
2 garlic cloves
½ bunch of mint, chopped
salt

Heat a small frying pan and gently toast the pine nuts, shaking occasionally, until they're golden brown, then allow to cool.

Cook the peas in a pan of boiling salted water for a few minutes until cooked, then run under a cold tap to refresh. Roughly chop and set to one side.

Cook the broad beans in a pan of boiling salted water for around 12–15 minutes until soft, then run under a cold tap to refresh. Peel and discard the skins then roughly chop.

Place the pine nuts, basil, Parmesan, olive oil and garlic in a food processor and blitz into a fine, smooth paste. Place into a large bowl and gently fold in the chopped peas, beans and mint.

Season to taste, then bottle the pesto in a sterilised jar. Store in the fridge and use within 2 weeks.

Parma Ham and Mozzarella Pizza Tin

Girls, if you ever want to get the seal of approval of your boyfriend's nearest and dearest, this is the recipe. Nice and simple to make, and perfect for them celebrating or commiserating the match results. Serve with a winning smile, hot red lippy, lots of beer and then leave the room. His mates will be in awe and it won't be long before he's putting a ring on it!

SERVES 6–8

FOR THE PIZZA DOUGH
30g fresh yeast (or 1 tablespoon
    active dried yeast)
260ml warm water
500g strong white flour, sifted
1 teaspoon sugar
small pinch of salt

FOR THE FILLING
2 tablespoons tomato purée
8 slices of Parma ham
50g Parmesan cheese, grated
100g mozzarella cheese grated
10 basil leaves, torn

Dissolve the yeast in the warm water. Place the flour in a large mixing bowl, add the sugar, salt and yeast, then combine together using your hands until a dough forms – it should feel smooth and come away from the sides of the bowl.

Knead the dough on a floured work surface for 10 minutes until it is elastic. Place the dough back in the bowl, cover with clingfilm and leave to rise in a warm place for about 30 minutes until it has doubled in size.

Once the dough has risen, lightly flour the work surface again, remove the dough from the bowl and re-shape it into a ball, then roll out into a rectangle about 30 x 60cm. Spread the tomato purée evenly over the dough. Layer slices of Parma ham to cover the base, then scatter the grated Parmesan, mozzarella and torn basil leaves on top.

Roll the dough into a sausage shape – this should look like a Swiss roll. Cut into slices 5cm thick and place into a greased, round cake tin or pastry ring (25cm diameter, 5cm deep). Leave in a warm place to re-prove for about 30 minutes until they have doubled in size again.

Preheat the oven to 180°C/160°C Fan/Gas Mark 4.

Once the slices have risen, bake in the preheated oven for approximately 25 minutes or until golden brown. Allow to cool slightly before serving.

180°/160°/Gas Mark 4
20-25 mins

Chicken and Mushroom Pot Pies

Who doesn't love pie? These individual pots are oozing with rich creamy sauce. We've used a quirky cockerel-shaped cookie cutter and served in steel tins to decorate. Share and enjoy on the day of making.

SERVES 4

200g ready-made puff pastry
200g chicken breasts, diced
400ml chicken stock
40g butter
40g plain flour, sieved
100ml double cream
10ml olive oil
1 large shallot, sliced
2 garlic cloves, chopped
150g button mushrooms, sliced
salt and freshly ground black
 pepper
2 egg yolks, beaten, for glazing

Flour a work surface and roll out the pastry until about 2mm thick. Line 4 individual 200ml pie pots with the pastry (large ramekins or muffin tins will work just as well if you don't have small pie pots). Cut 4 pastry lids to top the pies using a round cutter or a large saucer that's slightly larger than the pots. Place the pots and pastry tops in the fridge for 30 minutes to rest.

Place the chicken and chicken stock in a saucepan over a low heat, bring to a gentle simmer and cook for 10 minutes. Once the chicken is cooked, remove with a slotted spoon, set to one side and leave the stock on a rolling boil.

In another saucepan, melt the butter gently over a low heat and stir in the flour to form a smooth paste, then whisk this mixture into the boiling stock to thicken it. Turn the heat down so the sauce is gently simmering and add the cream, stirring continuously as the sauce simmers for a further 5 minutes. Then take the saucepan off the heat and allow to cool to room temperature.

Heat the oil in a saucepan, add the shallot, garlic and mushrooms and fry until they have softened and are cooked. Season with salt and pepper. Add the mushroom mixture and cooked chicken to the sauce and allow to cool slightly.

Remove the pie pots and lids from the fridge and spoon in the chicken filling, but don't overfill. Brush the underside of the lids with beaten egg yolk and place them on top of the pies, crimping the edges to seal the pies properly. Brush the top of the lids with beaten egg to glaze, then pierce a small hole in the top of each pie with a sharp knife.

Package and keep chilled.

ON THE LABEL WRITE:
Preheat the oven to 180°C/160°C Fan/Gas Mark 4. Bake for 20–25 minutes until golden brown.

Orange, Whiskey and Dill Gravadlax

This is a real showstopper. The salmon takes a bit of effort but will be well appreciated; it's a marriage with this easy but delicious English mustard dressing and a perfect starter for a dinner party.

MAKES 1 SIDE OF SALMON

FOR THE SALMON
8 tablespoons coarse salt
8 tablespoons caster sugar
1 tablespoon cracked black pepper
1kg side of salmon, skin on and pin boned
1 orange, sliced
100ml whiskey
1 tablespoon olive oil
1 bunch of dill, finely chopped

FOR THE EASY ENGLISH MUSTARD SAUCE
2 tablespoons English mustard
2 tablespoons caster sugar
2 tablespoons white wine vinegar
8 tablespoons sunflower oil
salt and freshly ground black pepper

Mix the salt, sugar and black pepper together in a large bowl.

Take a deep-sided tray the length of the salmon fillet. Sprinkle half the salt and sugar mixture in the base, place the salmon skin side down in the tray, then pack the rest of the mixture on top, making sure you completely cover the salmon. Layer over with orange slices, then gently splash with whiskey. Wrap the tray in clingfilm and place in the fridge for 24 hours.

After 24 hours, unwrap and gently spoon any liquid that has come out of the salmon back over the fish and the orange slices. Re-wrap and leave in the fridge for a further 24 hours.

After the full 48 hours of curing, remove from the fridge. Discard the sugary liquid and oranges, rinse the salmon under cold running water and pat dry with kitchen paper.

Brush the salmon with olive oil and pack the freshly chopped dill on top. Place the salmon on a board, keep in the fridge and slice as needed. Eat within 7 days.

To make the accompanying dressing, place the mustard, sugar and vinegar in a bowl and whisk slowly, adding the oil until it emulsifies together. Season to taste and serve alongside the salmon.

Golden Chocolate Pots

Very glam, these look good and taste lovely. A great chocolate fix with a little boozy hit!
Garnished with fun chocolate spoons they make for a real treat.

MAKES 4

100g good-quality dark chocolate,
  finely chopped
250ml double cream
40g soft brown sugar
1 vanilla pod, seeds removed
1 teaspoon rock salt, plus extra to
  garnish
10ml Cointreau (optional)
1 egg
1 pinch rock salt, for garnishing
1 sheet of edible gold leaf paper

Place the chocolate in a large mixing bowl.

Place the cream, sugar, vanilla seeds, rock salt and Cointreau, if using, in a large, heavy-based saucepan, stir and gently bring to the boil. Once boiling, remove from the heat.

Pour the cream mixture over the chocolate and whisk until melted and well combined, then quickly whisk in the egg. Pour into small pots, allow to cool, then chill in the fridge until set. To finish, sprinkle with rock salt and edible gold leaf. Eat within 3 days.

Flowerpot Apple and Hazelnut Crumbles

Crumble is a favourite for us, it's quintessentially very British … and also very easy! Add a nice jug of fresh cream and you're good to go! Dig in and enjoy. For some serious brownie points on style, try putting these into small clay flowerpots (new ones, from your local garden centre) for individual portions. For big family-style service, serve in a deep dish enamel tin.

MAKES 12 MINI FLOWERPOTS

50g butter
8 Granny Smith apples, peeled, cored and chopped into 2.5cm cubes
1 teaspoon ground cinnamon
40g golden caster sugar
juice of ½ lemon
½ teaspoon vanilla extract
12 disks of white bread, cut to fit in the base of your flowerpots (to cover the hole in the base)
12 sprigs of thyme

FOR THE TOPPING

100g brown demerara sugar
125g butter, softened
150g plain flour, sifted
50g hazelnuts, chopped

Melt the 50g butter in a heavy-based saucepan over a medium heat. Add the apple cubes, cinnamon, caster sugar, lemon juice and vanilla extract, then cook, stirring frequently, for 10–15 minutes or until the apples are softened but still holding their shape. Allow to cool.

For the topping, mix the brown sugar, butter, flour and hazelnuts between your fingers gently until you have a sand-like texture.

Place a small disc of white bread at the base of each flowerpot to plug the hole. Fill the flowerpots three-quarters of the way up with the cooled apple mixture, then finish with a layer of the hazelnut topping,

Garnish with a sprig of fresh thyme.

PLACE IN A BOX AND LABEL WITH THE FOLLOWING:
Cook me for 30 minutes at 180°C/160°C Fan/Gas Mark 4 without my thyme stalk (or it might burn), then replace to garnish. Eat me within 2 days.

Chapter Four:
Sweet Treats

These are essential presents for anyone with a sweet tooth, and perfect gifts for any special occasions like a birthday, holiday or any other day really…

There are big jars or trays of Chocolate and Honeycomb Pistachio Shards, Raspberry Meringue Kisses and Chocolate Swirly Lollies. We had a lot of fun inventing our Dirty Ice – a play on the classic pink and white coconut ice. We turned the pink to grey and added some sparkle and it reminds us of the driven snow in winter time, making it perfect for a Christmas gift. Lastly, those Polenta, Almond and Citrus Bars make a stunning gift with all the warmth of the beautiful Mediterranean.

Enjoy giving these sweet treats, guaranteed to get you a big grin every time!

Chocolate Hazelnut Fudge

If you can bag these before everyone eats them, you've had a result! Wrap these salty sweet explosions and take them to a dinner party – they're perfect with coffee and a brandy.

MAKES 30–40 PIECES

397g tin of condensed milk
150ml double cream
450g demerara sugar
115g butter
2 tablespoons chocolate hazelnut
    spread
hazelnuts and coarse sea salt, for
    garnishing

Line a 20 x 20cm baking tin with baking parchment.

Place all the ingredients except the hazelnuts and sea salt in a heavy-based saucepan. Stir and bring to the boil, then turn down the heat and simmer for 12–15 minutes, stirring continuously. If you have a sugar thermometer, the mixture should reach 115°C (soft ball stage); otherwise drop a small ball of the mixture into a bowl of iced water and see if it produces a soft ball.

Remove from the heat and beat for 3–4 minutes until thick. The fudge will set as it cools, so while it is still slightly warm and fluid, pour it into the lined baking tray. Decorate with hazelnuts, ensuring even spacing so you have a hazelnut on each round after cutting, then sprinkle with salt. Allow to cool, then cut into rounds.

Chocolate and Pistachio Honeycomb Shards

These are so luxe! Golden chunks, chocolate covered and then dipped in pistachio crumbs – elegant, stunning and almost too good to share!

SERVES 4–6

100g caster sugar
4 tablespoons golden syrup
1½ teaspoons bicarbonate of soda
250g good-quality dark chocolate
50g shelled pistachios, roughly chopped

Line a baking tray with baking parchment.

Put the sugar and golden syrup in a heavy-based saucepan and mix to make a paste, then slowly melt over a low to medium heat until the mixture reaches 150°C or the hard crack stage on a sugar thermometer.

Take the pan off the heat and quickly beat in the bicarbonate of soda using a wooden spoon – take care as the mixture will froth up to make honeycomb. Quickly pour the honeycomb onto the lined baking tray and allow to set at room temperature. Once set, remove the baking parchment and smash the honeycomb into shards.

Melt the chocolate in a heatproof bowl set over a saucepan of simmering water, making sure the water does not touch the base of the bowl. Once melted, stir the chocolate then dip the smashed honeycomb in it, sprinkle with chopped pistachios and leave to set on silicone paper.

Sparkling Salted Caramel

A staple in our home, we always seem to have a jar of this for our kids who love drizzling it on pretty much everything. Perfect slightly warmed for shortbread dunkers or cooled and sandwiched between biscuits or poured over ice cream… We could go on. Naughty but oh so nice!

MAKES 2 MEDIUM JARS

240g unsalted butter
240g light muscovado sugar
200ml double cream
1–2 teaspoons sea salt
½ teaspoon edible glitter

Melt the butter and sugar together in a saucepan over a low heat. When the mixture turns golden brown, take it off the heat and very carefully whisk in the cream.

Add the salt – taste after adding 1 teaspoon to see if it is salty enough for your taste; if not, add more. Stir in the glitter and allow the mixture to cool a little, then pour into sterilised jam jars. Seal and pop into the fridge to thicken.

Dirty Ice

We tend to give these out at Christmas as they look just like driven snow! They look so cute in a pretty vintage jar sprinkled with edible glitter.

MAKES 16–24 PIECES

500g icing sugar
397g tin of condensed milk
400g desiccated coconut
1 vanilla pod, split and seeds
    reserved
black food colouring
½ teaspoon edible silver glitter

Line a 20 x 20cm baking tin with clingfilm.

Sift the icing sugar into a large bowl, add the condensed milk, coconut and vanilla seeds, then mix well with gloved hands (this mix will be dry and tight so you really have to get stuck in).

Divide the mixture in half. Press one half into the bottom of the tin in an even layer.

Add a few drops of black food colouring to the remaining half and mix until thoroughly distributed and grey in colour. Carefully spread and press the grey mixture on top of the white to form an even layer.

Place in the fridge to set for 2 hours, then sprinkle with edible silver glitter and cut into squares.

Sesame Nut Brittle

We're nutty about nuts and think you will be too after this!

SERVES 4

300g caster sugar
2 tablespoons liquid glucose
50g unsalted peanuts, roughly
  chopped
50g unsalted cashews, roughly
  chopped
50g pistachios, roughly chopped
25g sesame seeds

Line a baking tray with baking parchment.

Pour the sugar and glucose into a heavy-based saucepan and place over a low heat. Shake the pan gently but do not stir. When the sugar and glucose have dissolved, increase the heat to medium-high and cook for 8–10 minutes until you have a nice golden brown caramel, shaking the pan gently throughout.

Add the nuts and seeds to the caramel and stir swiftly, then quickly pour onto the lined tray. Try to get an even layer of brittle (you may need to spread it with a lightly oiled metal spoon). Leave to set and go cold, then use a rolling pin to smash into pieces.

GROW YOUR OWN

Chocolate Swirly Lollies

These are so easy and so much fun. Try blitzing chocolate Oreo biscuits into fine crumbs and fill flowerpots to make edible soil, then 'plant' the chocolate flowers and watch them grow.

MAKES 18

100g each of milk chocolate, dark
  chocolate and white chocolate
20g dried cranberries
20g dried apricots, chopped
40g shelled pistachios, chopped
edible gold dust
18 wooden skewers

Melt the milk, dark and white chocolate in 3 separate heatproof bowls, each set over a pan of simmering water until silky and smooth. Do not let the water touch the base of the bowls. Remove from the heat and allow to cool slightly (around 5–10 minutes).

Line a baking tray with baking parchment. Place the wooden skewers on the baking parchment 7cm apart. Pour the melted chocolate into 3 piping bags and trim the ends with scissors so the chocolate pours out in a thin consistent line.

Pipe chocolate circles over each skewer again and again until you've got a perfect lollipop. Make sure the wooden skewers are in the centre of the piped circles and well covered with chocolate. You should be able to make a minimum of 18 lollipops. Before the chocolate sets, sprinkle with the cranberries, apricots, pistachios and edible gold dust.

Chill the tray of lollipops in the fridge. When set, gently peel the baking parchment off each lollipop.

Raspberry Meringue Kisses

Pucker up for these little beauties! Give to someone you love in a stylish apothecary glass jar.

MAKES 30

240g caster sugar, plus extra for
  dusting
4 egg whites
¼ teaspoon good-quality bright
  red gel food colour
1 tablespoon seedless raspberry
  jam
1 tablespoon finely chopped
  pistachios

Preheat the oven to 100°C/80°C Fan/Gas Mark ½. Line a baking tray with baking parchment and dust with a little caster sugar.

Whisk the egg whites in a food mixer until they form soft peaks. Continue whisking and slowly add half the sugar, making sure it is thoroughly incorporated into the egg whites.

Remove the bowl from the mixer and very slowly fold in the rest of the sugar using a large metal spoon. You should end up with a raw meringue that is thick and silky in texture and has a glossy sheen.

Add the gel food colour to the raspberry jam and mix together. Using a fork, gently drag the jam mixture through the meringue to marble, but do not over-mix.

Using a tablespoon, drop spoonfuls of the meringue onto the lined baking tray, then sprinkle the tops with finely chopped pistachios. Bake in the preheated oven for 1 hour or until the meringues lift easily off the baking parchment. Cool on a wire rack.

Polenta, Almond and Citrus Bars

Little slices of Sicilian heaven! Cut into bars, wrap half the bar in silicone paper and tie with dried citrus fruit and string.

MAKES 16–20

80g butter, melted, plus extra for greasing
1 vanilla pod, split and seeds reserved
5 eggs
100ml double cream
zest of 1 lemon, 1 orange and 1 lime
juice of 1 lime
300g caster sugar
pinch of sea salt
150g plain flour
½ teaspoon baking powder
50g polenta
40g ground almonds

FOR THE GLAZE
juice of 1 lemon and 1 orange
300g icing sugar

Preheat the oven to 180°C/160°C Fan/Gas Mark 4. Lightly butter a 30 x 20cm baking tin and line with baking parchment.

Place the melted butter, vanilla seeds, eggs, cream, zest, lime juice, sugar and salt in a large mixing bowl and whisk together.

Sift the flour and baking powder into the mixture, add the polenta and ground almonds, then whisk thoroughly until you have a smooth batter. Pour into the lined tin, place in the preheated oven and bake for 35–45 minutes. To test, insert a knife into the cake; the blade should come out clean.

Remove the cake from the oven, turn out on a wire rack and leave to cool.

To make the glaze, mix together the lemon and orange juice and the icing sugar, whisking until smooth.

Cut the cake into 16–20 bars and leave on the wire rack. Liberally spoon the glaze over the bars until all of it has been used.

Chapter Five:
With Love

Eight recipes for gifts straight from the heart with so much warmth and love. Show someone you really care and take some time out to make things, bake things and drape things in chocolate. It could very well end in the perfect 'Date Night' for you!

Enjoy giving, then making up the blinis together in the Smoked Salmon Blini Love Kit, then onto the Palmier Cinnamon Sugar Hearts, finally finishing with the Coconut and Raspberry Twists with Molten Chocolate Sauce. Mmmm…

A tactile bunch of gifts that involves audience participation. Enjoy!

Smoked Salmon Blini Love Kit

A bottle of bubbly, a cosy blanket and a warm summer breeze are the perfect combination to set the mood for romance with the one you love. This recipe will make too many blinis for two, but make them all and then freeze what you don't need for another impromptu romantic rendezvous!

MAKES 32

100g plain flour
pinch of salt
2 eggs
150ml milk
1 x 7g packet of active dried yeast
oil, for frying

FOR THE TOPPING/IN THE PACKAGE
100g good-quality smoked
   salmon, sliced (for 16 blinis)
100ml crème fraîche
1 small bunch of dill

Sift the flour into a mixing bowl and add the salt. Separate the eggs. Place the yolks in the bowl of flour. Place the egg whites in a clean bowl and put to one side for now.

Place the milk in a saucepan and gently warm to 37°C. Remove the pan from the heat and whisk in the yeast. Pour the milk and yeast into the flour and egg yolks, then mix to form a smooth batter. Cover and leave in a warm place to rise for 1 hour.

Whisk the egg whites to form soft peaks. Gently fold into the batter to make a light and fluffy mix.

Warm a frying pan over a medium heat, add the oil, then tablespoon the blini batter into the pan to form small pancakes. Flip to brown on both sides (cook for approximately 2 minutes per side), then remove and drain on kitchen paper. Repeat until you've used all the batter.

Beautifully package your blinis next to the sliced smoked salmon, jar of crème fraîche and dill. Add a teaspoon and have fun together building!

Coconut and Raspberry Twists with Molten Chocolate Sauce

Time to get sexy and a little messy! Dunk these delightful coconutty sticks into the warmed chocolate before popping into your mouth whilst gazing at your heart's desire seductively. If that doesn't get your lover's heart racing, the boozy hit from the Malibu will!

MAKES 16–20

200g shop-bought puff pastry
plain flour, for dusting
3 tablespoons raspberry jam
1 tablespoon water
40g good-quality soft dessicated
   coconut

FOR THE DIPPING SAUCE
150g dark chocolate, chopped
25g butter, cubed
1 tablespoon honey
1 tablespoon Malibu or rum

Line a baking tray with baking parchment.

Roll out the puff pastry on a floured work surface to measure 16 x 16cm, with a thickness of 5mm, then cut into strips 1cm wide.

Place the raspberry jam in a small saucepan with a tablespoon of water over a low heat. Gently warm and stir until the jam has melted and has mixed with the water, then allow to cool for 5 minutes. Brush the cooled jam over the pastry strips and sprinkle over the desiccated coconut. Hold each end of a strip and twist to form a spiral shape. Place on the lined baking tray 5mm apart and allow to rest in the fridge for 30 minutes.

Preheat the oven to 170°C/150°C Fan/Gas Mark 3½.

Place the baking tray in the preheated oven and bake for 15 minutes until golden brown. Cool on a wire rack.

To make the dip, place the chopped chocolate in a heatproof bowl with butter and honey. Place over a pan of simmering water on a medium heat and melt the chocolate slowly, stirring occasionally. Do not let the simmering water touch the base of the bowl. Once the chocolate has melted, gently stir in the Malibu or rum, but do not over mix. Decant into a container ready for dipping (if necessary, you can reheat the dip in the microwave for just a few seconds).

Boozy Chocolate Truffles

Prepare to get a little messy while rolling these, but they are worth it.

MAKES 30

300ml double cream
40g unsalted butter
300g dark chocolate (70%
   cocoa), chopped into large
   chunks
finely grated zest of 1 orange
1 teaspoon rock salt
1 tablespoon whiskey or dark rum
3 tablespoons cocoa powder
3 tablespoons pistachios,
   chopped
3 tablespoons good-quality soft
   desiccated coconut

Pour the cream into a heavy-based saucepan and gently warm over a low heat. Drop in the butter, bring to a slow simmer and stir until melted, then remove from the heat.

Place the chocolate in a large mixing bowl. Pour the warm cream mixture over the chocolate and stir until the chocolate has melted to a smooth texture. Fold in the orange zest, salt and alcohol, then place the bowl in the fridge to cool for 4–6 hours.

Take a large melon baller and dip it in hot water to heat. Use it to scoop the chocolate truffle mixture into balls, then place on silicone paper. While the outer chocolate is still melted, roll the truffles in cocoa powder, chopped pistachios or coconut, or all three! Re-shape between the palms of your hands if needed.

Place the truffles in the fridge to set.

True Love Brownie and Flapjack Squares

These have to be made to be believed! You get the lovely chewy oats of the flapjack and then bam! Rich dark chocolate from the brownie melts in your mouth. When I made these, suddenly the generous spirit in the house diminished and the family wasn't so keen on giving these away. Try them and see for yourself how good they are!

MAKES 28

FOR THE FLAPJACK
150g unsalted butter
150g soft brown sugar
140g golden syrup
325g porridge oats
100g mixed dried fruits of your
   choice

FOR THE BROWNIES
2 eggs
225g caster sugar
140g unsalted butter
60g dark cocoa powder
60g plain flour, sifted
40g dark chocolate chips
   (optional)

Preheat the oven to 150°C/130°C Fan/Gas Mark 2. Line a 20 x 32cm baking tray with baking parchment.

Start by making the flapjack layer. Place the butter, sugar and golden syrup in a pan and melt together over a gentle heat, stirring. Do not let the mixture boil. When melted, add the porridge oats and mixed fruits. Make sure they are fully mixed in with the wet ingredients, then put to one side.

For the brownie layer, whisk the eggs and sugar together in a bowl until slightly thickened, then place to one side. Melt the butter in a saucepan, then remove from the heat and whisk in the cocoa powder. Add the butter mixture to the eggs and sugar and gently mix until fully incorporated, then fold in the sifted flour and chocolate chips, if using.

Spread the flapjack mixture on the base of the lined baking tray and press down gently so the top is nice and even. The pour the brownie mix on top and level the surface with a spatula.

Bake in the preheated oven for 35–40 minutes until cooked. The brownie will crack slightly on top when cooked.

Leave to cool completely before turning out of the tray. Cut into 5cm squares and serve.

Chocolate-draped Strawberries

These, a little bit of background music from the 'Walrus of Love' and a good bottle of champagne are the perfect three ingredients for a very romantic canoodling!

MAKES 25–30

150g good-quality white
   chocolate, chopped
150g good-quality dark chocolate,
   chopped
1 large punnet (400–500g)
   strawberries

Place the white and dark chocolate in separate heatproof bowls. Place each bowl over a pan of simmering water, making sure that the water does not touch the base of the bowls, and let the chocolate melt. Gently stir until silky smooth, then remove from the heat.

Pour half the white chocolate and half the dark chocolate into two separate piping bags. Dip a strawberry three-quarters deep into the remaining dark chocolate and place on silicone paper. While still melted, pipe a small dot of white chocolate onto the dark chocolate-coated strawberry, then quickly take the tip of a skewer or knife and draw it down through the white chocolate dot to make a heart. Leave the chocolate to set. Repeat with the remaining strawberries, dipping half in the dark chocolate and half in the white.

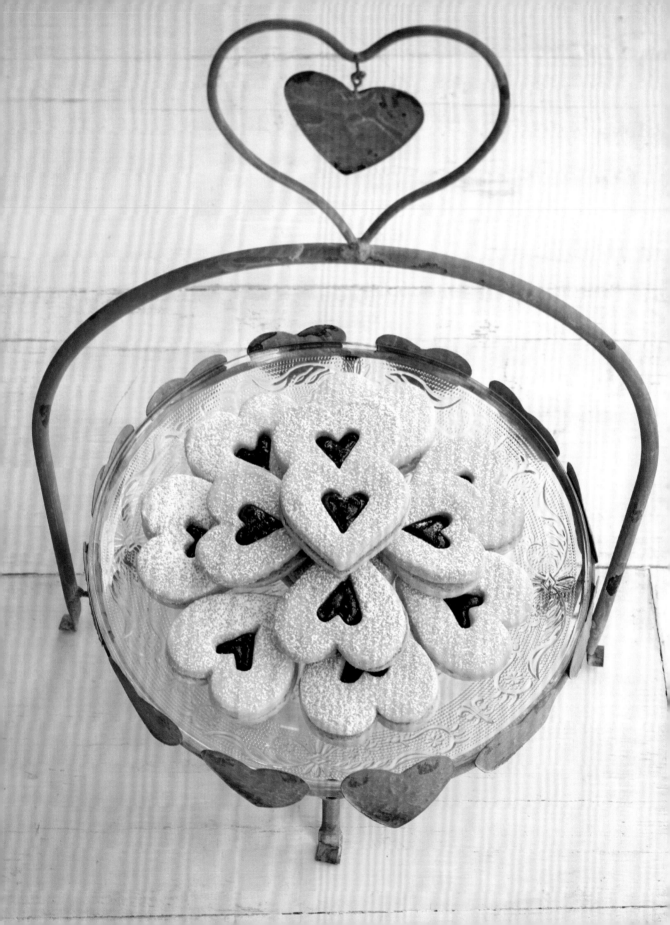

Jammy Hearts

We've pimped up this popular British treat by using shortbread mix for the biscuit. They melt in your mouth and are sure to melt your lover's heart!

MAKES 6

100g butter, cubed and softened
150g plain flour, sifted
50g caster sugar
2 drops vanilla extract
3 tablespoons seedless raspberry
   jam
icing sugar, for dusting

Rub the butter into the flour until it resembles fine breadcrumbs, then fold in the sugar and add the vanilla extract. Work the mixture until it forms a smooth ball and leaves the sides of the bowl clean. Cover the dough with clingfilm and refrigerate for 1 hour.

Preheat the oven to 140°C/120°C Fan/Gas Mark 1. Line a baking tray with baking parchment.

Remove the dough from the fridge and allow it to come up to room temperature. Lightly flour a work surface and roll the dough out until it is 1cm thick. Using a heart-shaped cutter, cut out 12 hearts. Using a smaller heart-shaped cutter, cut the middle out of 6 of the hearts—these will be the biscuit tops.

Place all the biscuits on the lined baking tray and bake in the preheated oven for 30 minutes or until they are a very pale gold colour. Using a spatula or fish slice, carefully transfer to a wire rack, then dust with icing sugar when cooled.

Spoon the raspberry jam generously over the 6 biscuit bases. Place the tops on the biscuits and dust with icing sugar.

Red Fruit Jelly Champagne Flutes

Anything with Champagne in it gets our vote and our heart!

SERVES 6

4 leaves of gelatine
400ml Champagne or sparkling
 wine
250g mixed red fruits

Place the gelatine in a bowl of cold water and soak until soft.

Pour half the Champagne or sparkling wine in a saucepan and warm gently. Drain the gelatine leaves and squeeze out any excess water, then drop them into the warm Champagne and slowly stir until melted.

Remove the pan from the heat and allow to the mixture to cool, then add the rest of the Champagne and gently stir. Divide the mixed red fruits between 6 Champagne glasses, then top up with Champagne jelly.

Refrigerate for 3 hours to set, then package with love.

Palmier Cinnamon Sugar Hearts

These are also called Elephant's Ears, but Palmier Hearts sounds much nicer and more fitting for a romantic gesture!

MAKES 16–18

320g shop-bought puff pastry
2 egg yolks, beaten
50g demerara sugar
½ teaspoon ground cinnamon
plain flour, for dusting

Roll the puff pastry out to a rectangle 20 x 30cm and 5mm thick, then brush with some of the beaten egg yolk.

Thoroughly mix the sugar and cinnamon together, then sprinkle over the pastry right up to the edges, reserving a little sugar for the tops. From the long edge, roll the pastry up tightly to the centre, then repeat from the opposite side to form a heart-shaped roll. Wrap in clingfilm and refrigerate for 1 hour.

Preheat the oven to 180°C/160°C Fan/Gas Mark 4. Line a baking tray with silicone paper.

Dust the blade of a sharp knife with flour. Working on a floured work surface, cut the pastry roll into slices 1cm thick. Place on the lined baking tray, allowing room for them to double in size. Brush with egg yolk and sprinkle with a little more cinnamon sugar.

Bake in the preheated oven for 12–15 minutes until golden brown. Leave to cool on a wire rack.

Chapter Six:
Healthy Goodies

A big chapter and rightly so as it's snuggled between lots of not so pure, sweet and savoury neighbouring chapters. Enjoy making, wrapping and showing someone you really care about them and their welfare with any of this healthy lot.

We start with super-healthy and tasty Nature's Bounty Power Drinks, giving the gift of health by blitzing and getting the recipient to glug straight away to capture all those vitamins. As for the Powerhouse Granola, it's simply bake and bag – it won't stay in there for long, I promise you. The Slow-burn Porridge Pots are a true, slow-energy releasing gem. Make a week's supply in advance, pot and give to your busy family. Just add fresh milk and ping and ding in the microwave, perfect when you're running late in the morning! Both the Root Vegetable Crisp Bags and Dried Fruit Sweet Bags are a healthier take on their naughtier cousins – try to get the kids onto these and you've cracked it!

Nature's Bounty Power Drinks

*You may have heard the saying to 'Eat the rainbow', well now you can drink the rainbow!
The great thing about these juices is you can very speedily pack a lot of veggies and
nature's good stuff into your system, providing you with a quick vitamin hit!*

EACH DRINK MAKES 300ML

WORKOUT WONDER
2.5cm piece cucumber
½ celery stick
½ apple
3 teaspoons lemon juice
6 mint leaves
100ml fresh apple juice
3 ice cubes

MORNING GLORY
¼ apple
1 carrot
10g ginger
½ orange
100ml apple juice
3 ice cubes

DETOX
½ apple
½ small carrot
1½ teaspoons lemon juice
1cm piece cucumber
¼ celery stick
1 teaspoon linseeds
2 stems parsley
¼ small beetroot
¼ small avocado
100ml fresh apple juice
3 ice cubes

Blitz all ingredients for your chosen power drink in a blender and pass
through a strainer. Pour into a sterilised bottle and seal.

ADD A LABEL SAYING:
Drink me now!

Powerhouse Granola

Warning: this is very moreish! Packed with nuts and superfruits for an unbeatable way to start your day, the addition of cinnamon will get your metabolism fired up and ready to take on the day. Perfect with Greek yoghurt or a splash of cold almond milk.

SERVES 10

50ml vegetable oil
3 tablespoons water
250ml organic honey

DRY INGREDIENTS
300g oats
50g pecans, broken
50g pistachios, roughly chopped
60g flaked almonds
50g pumpkin seeds
50g sunflower seeds
25g sesame seeds
3 teaspoons ground cinnamon

DRIED FRUITS
70g sultanas
50g apricots, chopped
50g golden berries
50g dried cranberries
40g goji berries
50g dried blueberries

Preheat the oven to 150°C/130°C Fan/Gas Mark 2. Line 2 baking trays with baking parchment.

Mix all the dry ingredients together in a bowl. Gently warm the oil, water and honey in a small saucepan until mixture becomes runny. Pour the honey mixture over the dry ingredients and stir thoroughly with a wooden spoon; the mixture will be very sticky. Spread the mixture over the 2 trays in a thin, even layer. Bake in the preheated oven for approximately 30 minutes until golden brown, making sure you turn the mixture every 5–10 minutes.

When you remove the trays from the oven, the mixture will still seem quite soft but as it cools it will begin to harden. While it is still warm, mix in the dried fruit, then leave to cool.

Once cool, store in an airtight container.

'Just Add Milk' Slow-burn Porridge Pots

Another great start to the day is this slow-energy releasing super porridge. Both porridge and granola stand proudly together, making a superfood breakfast hero.

SERVES 4

25g hazelnuts, chopped
25g pecans, chopped
25g pistachios, shelled and
    chopped
25g pumpkin seeds
25g golden berries
25g dried cranberries
340g porridge oats

TO SERVE
1 litre skimmed milk
4 tablespoons organic honey

Preheat the oven to 160°C/140°C Fan/Gas Mark 3.

Place all the nuts and pumpkin seeds on a baking tray and roast in the preheated oven for 10 minutes, then allow to cool. Mix the cooled nuts with the dried fruits and porridge oats, then divide the mixture between four 300ml lidded pots.

TIE A LABEL TO EACH POT, WITH THE FOLLOWING INFORMATION:
Add 250ml milk to each pot and place in a high-powered microwave for 1½–2 minutes, stirring halfway through. Drizzle a tablespoon of honey over each pot and enjoy.

Oil-free Raw and Rich Super Salad Dressing

This is a super-easy dressing – it really is just a blitz and you're ready to go. Sublime drizzled over a spiced chickpea salad.

MAKES 500ML

2 tablespoons tahini
1 tablespoon white wine vinegar
juice of 1 lemon
½ bunch of flat-leaf parsley,
   chopped
2 garlic cloves, chopped
1 tablespoon organic honey
200ml coconut water
150ml natural probiotic yoghurt
salt and freshly ground black
   pepper

Place all ingredients into a blender and blitz together until smooth and thoroughly incorporated. Season to taste. Pour into a sterilised jar and label.

Super Fruit and Coconut Milk Sushi

A novel way of getting fruit into some of the fussiest of eaters. This was road-tested on a friend's toddler and it was a pleasure seeing them go back for lozenge after lozenge. Not just for the younger ones, this makes a great start to the day or a perfectly light dessert after a spicy Asian feast.

MAKES 16

250g sushi rice
330ml water
60g caster sugar
120ml unsweetened coconut milk
8 physalis
12 blueberries
1 fig, sliced into 8
1 blood orange, peeled and sliced

Wash the rice under cold running water 2–3 times. Pour the water into a large saucepan, add the rice and bring it to the boil over a medium heat. Cover the saucepan with a lid and simmer the rice for about 10 minutes until all the water has been absorbed. Remove the rice from the heat and leave it to cool in the pan for 10–15 minutes – it will continue to swell and at the same time get sticky as its temperature drops.

Warm the sugar and coconut milk in a saucepan over a medium heat, stirring until all the sugar has dissolved. Add the milk to the pan of rice and once again leave the rice to absorb the liquid.

Line a deep-sided baking tray (20cm long x 15cm wide x 2cm deep) with clingfilm, allowing the edges of the clingfilm to overlap the rim. Spread the rice evenly in the tray, packing it down, then pop it into the fridge for 2–3 hours. Once the rice has set firmly, remove it from the fridge and use the overlapping clingfilm to lift it out of the tray onto your work surface.

Using a sharp knife dipped in water, cut the rice into 16 rectangles of equal length (4cm long x 2cm wide). Arrange the fruit on top of the rice bites and serve the super fruit sushi.

High Energy Bars

Perfect for your friends or family who are always rushed off their feet. Alongside the Bliss Energy Balls, their slow-releasing energy keeps you going throughout the day and are brimming with natural goodness.

MAKES 8

125g light muscovado sugar
90g unsalted butter
90g organic honey
175g oats
25g sunflower seeds
25g sesame seeds
25g flaked almonds
25g ground almonds
40g dried sour cherries, chopped
40g dried blueberries
40g dried apricots, chopped

Preheat the oven to 160°C/140°C Fan/Gas Mark 3. Line a 20 x 15cm baking tray with baking parchment.

Place the sugar, butter and honey in a saucepan and slowly melt over a low heat. Mix all remaining ingredients together in a large bowl.

Once the butter mixture has melted, pour it over the dry ingredients, mixing everything thoroughly until you have a sticky mixture. Tip the mixture into the lined tray, patting it down to an even thickness.

Bake in the preheated oven for 20–25 minutes until it turns golden brown, then allow to cool before cutting into 8 bars.

Bliss Energy Balls

I make these every Sunday and throughout the week we all dig in, whether it be for a boost before the gym or a little go-to before dinner. The chia seeds are great as they swell inside your tum, giving you that satisfied feeling without the guilt.

MAKES 20–24

12 tablespoons oatmeal
8 tablespoons peanut butter
6 tablespoons honey
6 tablespoons flax seeds
1 tablespoon chia seeds
6 Medjool dates, stoned and
    chopped
1 tablespoon dried blueberries

TO ROLL
8 tablespoons desiccated
    coconut
4 tablespoons pistachios, finely
    chopped

Place the oatmeal, peanut butter, honey, flax seeds, chia seeds, dates and blueberries in a blender and blitz for 2–3 minutes to a grainy paste consistency, regularly scraping down the sides of the blender. Roll into small balls of around 20g.

Mix together the desiccated coconut and chopped pistachios on a plate. Roll the balls in this mix, then in your hands to stick the pistachio and coconut onto the outside of the balls.

Store in a tight-fitting container.

Chunky Tomato Super Soup

The Mediterranean in a bowl, this soup is surprisingly filling and packed full of goodness. This works really well with a little dollop of the Chunky Bean and Pea Pesto (see page 51) on top.

SERVES 6

1 red onion, roughly chopped
3 garlic cloves, roughly chopped
½ red pepper, roughly chopped
500g plum tomatoes, roughly chopped
15ml olive oil
700ml vegetable stock
35g baby spinach, shredded
200g courgettes, diced into 1cm cubes
50g Puy lentils, cooked (or 35g uncooked – cook according to the packet instructions)
salt and freshly ground black pepper

Preheat the oven to 160°C/140°C Fan/Gas Mark 3.

Place the red onion, garlic, red pepper and plum tomatoes in a baking tray, drizzle with olive oil and roast in the preheated oven for about 30 minutes until soft. Once soft, transfer to a heavy-based pan over a medium heat and pour in the vegetable stock. Bring to the boil, then reduce the heat and simmer, uncovered, for a further 20 minutes.

Season with salt and pepper, then blend the soup using a stick blender until smooth. Return the pan to the heat, bring back to the boil and add the spinach, courgette and cooked lentils. Cook for around 3 minutes until the courgette is tender.

If packaging as a gift, allow to cool then pour into a container.

ADD A LABEL SAYING:
Pour into a pan, bring to the boil and serve.

Pho to Go!

One of our favourite adventures was discovering the beautiful land of Vietnam. Whilst there we enjoyed the most amazing soups for lunch by the beach – bursting with flavour and not too heavy on the calories, this is a recipe that sends us straight back to that wonderful place, with its chaotic traffic, immense love of sounding their horns and traffic-stopping smiles.

MAKES 4 X 300ML POTS

2 litres beef stock

30g fresh ginger, peeled and chopped

1 onion, finely chopped

3 garlic cloves, chopped

3 star anise

1 cinnamon stick (10cm)

1 teaspoon nam prik pau chilli paste

2 tablespoons fish sauce

½ bunch of coriander, chopped (root and stem)

300g fillet beef, sliced into 1cm strips

100g flat rice noodles

180g bean sprouts

1 red chilli, deseeded and sliced

½ bunch of spring onions, chopped

2 tablespoons sweet basil, torn

2 tablespoons mint, torn

2 tablespoons coriander leaves, torn

First make the pho stock. Place the beef stock in a saucepan over a high heat with the ginger, onion, garlic, star anise, cinnamon stick, chilli paste, fish sauce and chopped coriander. Bring to the boil, then turn the heat down and simmer, uncovered, for 30 minutes. Remove from the heat.

Place the beef strips in a large bowl, then strain the hot pho stock over the top – this will slowly cook the meat. Allow to cool to room temperature.

Place the noodles in boiling water as per the packet instructions until soft (about 10 minutes), then drain.

Divide the drained noodles and 150g of bean sprouts between 4 lidded pots. Remove the beef strips from the stock with a slotted spoon and divide between the pots. Mix the beef, noodles and bean sprouts together, then carefully top up each pot with the pho stock.

To finish, garnish each pot with the remaining bean sprouts, chilli, spring onions and torn herbs.

Cover the pots with their lids and place in the refrigerator to cool.

LABEL WITH THE FOLLOWING:
Ping and ding me in a high-powered microwave for 1½–2 minutes with my lid off. Then stir and enjoy me with some hot sauce.

Low-sugar Mixed Nut Cookies

Sugar seems to be the enemy of the moment, so we've tried to reduce the quantities and replaced it with unrefined brown sugar. These aren't complete saints but they're trying to be better than their sugar-laden counterparts. Stack these beautifully in a glass jar or select a stunning box and package with care and love.

MAKES 20–30

160g unsalted butter
8 level tablespoons powdered natural sweetener
150g light brown sugar
1 teaspoon vanilla extract
2 eggs
150g plain wholemeal flour
165g plain flour
¾ teaspoon bicarbonate of soda
½ teaspoon salt
100g shelled pistachios
100g hazelnuts, chopped
100g flaked almonds
60g walnuts, chopped

In a medium bowl, cream together the butter, sweetener and brown sugar until smooth. Stir in the vanilla extract and eggs.

In a separate bowl combine the wholemeal flour, plain flour, bicarbonate of soda and salt. Gradually blend the flour mixture into the creamed mixture. Fold in all the nuts. Leave to chill in the fridge for at least 1 hour.

Preheat the oven to 190°C/170°C Fan/Gas Mark 5. Grease 2 baking trays, or line with baking parchment.

Shape the mixture into small golf ball-sized pieces and gently press each one down on the baking trays. Leave space between each cookie as they will spread out as they bake.

Bake for 8–10 minutes in the preheated oven. Allow the cookies to cool on the baking trays for 5 minutes before removing to a wire rack to cool completely.

Root Vegetable Crisp Bags

These babies are baked not fried, so your friends can dig in with gusto and a clear conscience. We love putting these in paper sacks rolled down and filled to the brim.

MAKES 6 BAGS

1 large sweet potato
1 large parsnip
1 large beetroot
1 large carrot
2 teaspoons smoked paprika
3 tablespoons olive oil
rock salt

Preheat the oven to 120°C/100°C Fan/Gas Mark ¾. Line a baking tray with silicone paper.

Peel the vegetables using a mandolin, swivel peeler or very sharp knife. Slice diagonally into wafer-thin slices. Wash under cold running water in a colander, then pat completely dry on kitchen paper or a clean tea towel.

Place the vegetable slices in a mixing bowl or on a tray, add the oil and paprika and mix thoroughly to cover all the slices. Place the slices on the lined baking tray and spread out, ensuring they do not overlap each other (you may need to bake the slices in batches). Bake in the preheated oven for 1 hour, turning regularly until light and crisp.

Remove and drain on kitchen paper. Season with rock salt and once cold, bag up.

Dried Fruit Sweet Bags

We all crave a little sweetness from time to time and this is a great go-to when you need that fix. Drying out the fruit like this really intensifies the flavour. We do this when we are in Mallorca and leave them out in the blazing Spanish sun to dry out whilst we soak up the rays too!

MAKES 4 BAGS

½ mango, peeled
½ sweet small pineapple, peeled
6 large strawberries
1 large apple
juice of 1 lemon
icing sugar, for dusting (optional)

Preheat the oven to 80°C/60°C Fan/Gas Mark ¼, or your oven's lowest setting. Line a baking tray with silicone paper.

Using a very sharp knife or mandolin, carefully slice all the fruit into thin whole slices. Dip the apple slices into the lemon juice to keep them from discolouring.

Place the fruit on the lined baking tray, ensuring the slices do not touch each other. For shine, dust them with a little icing sugar, then place in the preheated oven. Dry the fruit slices for about 3 hours, turning them regularly until crisp.

Once dried, mix and bag the fruit for a healthy snack.

Gluten-free Carrot Flowerpot Muffins

With so many different dietary requirements, it would be criminal to leave out a decent recipe for those sensitive to gluten!

MAKES 8 MINI MUFFINS

2 eggs
100g brown sugar
100ml vegetable oil
zest of ½ orange
1 tablespoon orange juice
150g gluten-free self-raising flour
1 teaspoon ground cinnamon
125g finely grated carrot
50g sultanas

FOR THE FROSTING
500g low-fat cream cheese
250g icing sugar
zest of 2 lemons

Preheat the oven to 190°C/170°C Fan/Gas Mark 5. Line an 8-hole muffin tin with paper cases.

Beat together the eggs, sugar and oil, then mix in the orange zest and orange juice. Beat in the flour and cinnamon, then stir in the grated carrot and sultanas. Spoon the batter into the prepared tin and bake in the preheated oven for 20–25 minutes. Allow the muffins to cool in the tin.

To make the frosting, place the cream cheese in a bowl, sift in the icing sugar and mix well. Add the lemon zest, mix again and then spoon into a piping bag. Chill in the fridge for 30 minutes.

Decorate the muffins with frosting and marzipan carrots, and drop into your flowerpots.

Low-fat Greek Yoghurt Panna Cotta Pots

Waist-line friendly panna cottas! These delightful little pots are fabulous for sharing with the calorie conscious.

MAKES 8

5 gelatine leaves or sheets
200ml semi-skimmed milk
2 tablespoons organic honey
1 vanilla pod, split open and
   seeds scraped out
500g non-fat Greek yoghurt, at
   room temperature
blueberries, to serve

Place the gelatine leaves in cold water to soak for around 10 minutes. Drain and squeeze out any excess water.

Slowly heat the milk in a heavy-based saucepan to just below boiling. Whisk in the softened gelatine, then add the honey and vanilla seeds. Whisk together thoroughly, then remove from the heat – do not let this mixture boil. Allow to cool for 5 minutes.

Place the yoghurt in a large mixing bowl. While the milk mixture is still warm, slowly strain through a sieve into the yoghurt, whisking continuously until fully mixed together.

Pour into individual glasses and refrigerate for 3–4 hours until set. Serve with fresh blueberries.

Chapter Seven:
Al Fresco

Time to go outside and enjoy friendship and laughter. What would be really thoughtful and fun would be to take a delicious gift along with you, so here are some great picnic presents that will get you an invite to all the best garden parties.

Some of the recipes require a little on-the-spot assembly, such as the DIY Picnic Tomato, Burrata and Basil Pot, with the sweet tomatoes still on their truss, melting burrata and fresh basil in its pot, all crying out to be pulled, torn, chopped and finished with glugs of quality olive oil. Perfect alongside our Pork and Apple Scotch Eggs, Smoked Chicken, Apricot and Thyme Sausage Rolls and Steak and Mozzarella Wedge. Wrap in fun materials like muslin and linen and package in wicker baskets and wood boxes, all to be refrigerated and eaten on the day.

Lastly, finish it all off and get smashing those meringues, mixing with berries and shaking that cream in our Smash-it-up Picnic Eton Mess.

Smoked Chicken Big Caesar Jars

Perfect for a speedy Caesar when time is of the essence and you want to provide something tasty for those you love on the go. We've always found that if you package something beautifully or in a novel way, people are far more willing to try it.

MAKES 4

3 tablespoons olive oil, for frying
150g cubed pancetta
4 slices of white bread, cubed
4 tablespoons mayonnaise
2 garlic cloves, crushed
2 tablespoons chopped parsley
30g Parmesan cheese, finely grated
300g smoked cooked chicken breast, sliced
6 Baby Gem lettuces, chopped
50g Parmesan curls
salt and freshly ground black pepper

Heat the olive oil in a frying pan, add the pancetta cubes and fry until crispy, then remove and drain on kitchen paper.

Reheat the oil in the pan, add the cubes of bread and fry on all sides until crispy. Drain these croutons on kitchen paper.

To make the dressing, place the mayonnaise in a bowl and whisk in the garlic, parsley and grated Parmesan. Season and add a splash of cold water, whisking until the correct consistency. You may need about 5 tablespoons of water, but add gradually to avoid ending up with a sauce that is too thin.

Take 4 large jars with screw lids. Divide the chicken between the jars, then the pancetta. Add the lettuce, then top with croutons and Parmesan curls – the jars should be about three-quarters full.

Pour the Caesar dressing into small pots with lids and place on top of the salad in each jar. Screw the lids on tight – perfect for a picnic to pour, mix and enjoy.

Blood Orange, Feta and Pomegranate Slaw

Pretty as a picture and super fresh. This is a great salad while blood oranges are in season, but it works just as well with any other in-season oranges.

SERVES 6

125g feta cheese
1 large fennel bulb
3 blood oranges, peeled
1 pomegranate, deseeded
2 tablespoons chopped flat-leaf
  parsley
2 tablespoons olive oil
1 tablespoon molasses
salt and freshly ground black
  pepper

Break the feta into chunks and place in a large mixing bowl. Trim the fennel and cut in half, then remove and discard the root. Very finely slice the fennel with a sharp knife or a mandolin and add to the feta.

Cut the oranges into chunks, add to the fennel and feta, then add the pomegranate seeds, parsley, olive oil and molasses. Gently fold together, then season to taste.

DIY Picnic Tomato, Burrata and Basil Pot

The world's best tear and share! We are big lovers of family-style food sharing. The simplicity of this dish is what makes it so beautiful. The focus is all on the ingredients, so make sure to buy the best and perfectly ripe tomatoes.

SERVES 4–6

2 balls of burrata, wrapped in
  muslin
200g cherry vine tomatoes
1 pot of fresh basil
olive oil
balsamic vinegar
salt and freshly ground black
  pepper

Package on a big oval plate or bowl, when ready open the burrata and tear, cut tomatoes in half and tear fresh basil leaves. Gently mix together with glugs of olive oil, balsamic vinegar and finish with salt and ground black pepper.

Steak and Mozzarella Wedge

A work of art in itself and probably the tastiest sarnie ever! The Italians know how to eat and who are we to argue? This is the perfect picnic centrepiece.

SERVES 6–8

4 tablespoons olive oil
2 x 160g sirloin steaks
3 red peppers, quartered and de-seeded
1 large ball Pugliese bread (around 500g)
2 garlic cloves, chopped
2 tablespoons horseradish sauce
60g baby spinach
2 x 125g buffalo mozzarella, sliced into 1cm rounds
salt and freshly ground black pepper

Heat 1 tablespoon of olive oil in a chargrill pan. Season the steaks, then sear for 2 minutes on each side over a high heat. Remove from the pan and set aside.

Add another tablespoon of olive oil to the pan and allow to smoke, then add the peppers and gently chargrill until tender and soft. Remove from the pan and drain on kitchen paper.

Using a serrated knife, cut off the top third of the loaf. Using your hands, gently remove the soft dough from inside the loaf and the lid, leaving you with the crust intact (discard the dough or make breadcrumbs for another recipe).

Rub the inside of the loaf case with the remaining olive oil, the garlic and horseradish. Place half the red peppers in a layer to cover the bottom of the loaf case and season. Take half of the spinach and flatten it firmly on top of the peppers. Remember to season between each layer. Firmly press half the mozzarella on the spinach layer. Press the steaks firmly on the mozzarella layer. On top of the steaks add the second ball of sliced mozzarella, then pack on top the remaining spinach and finish with the remaining peppers. The layered ingredients will be overflowing, but don't worry as the lid will help to contain them.

Place the bread lid on top and tightly wrap the whole loaf several times with clingfilm. Place the wrapped loaf on a baking tray, place another baking tray over the top and weigh down with a large casserole dish or a heavy weight. Leave in the fridge for 3–4 hours for the loaf to press down.

To serve, remove the clingfilm and cut into wedges.

Goat's Cheese and Asparagus Bar Tart

If you can, use a beautiful rectangular tin mould for this. Of course it's not essential if you don't have one, but it makes for a far more contemporary look if you are giving as a gift.

SERVES 8–10

12 asparagus tips
3 eggs
1 teaspoon wholegrain mustard
2 tablespoons chopped parsley
375ml full-fat milk
125g goat's cheese, broken into
    small pieces
salt and freshly ground black
    pepper

FOR THE PASTRY
300g plain flour
pinch of salt
150g unsalted butter, diced
2 egg yolks
60ml ice-cold water

To make the pastry, sieve the flour and salt into a large mixing bowl. Add the butter and gently rub it into the flour using your fingertips until a fine crumb texture is achieved. Mix in the egg yolks and water. Knead into a dough, wrap in clingfilm and chill in the fridge for 1 hour.

Roll the pastry out to a thickness of 5mm. Lay over a greased oblong pastry tin (35 x 12cm), press into all corners and trim the excess pastry around the edges. Chill for 30 minutes.

Preheat the oven to 160°C/140°C Fan/Gas Mark 3.

Remove the pastry case from the fridge and fill with baking beans. Blind bake the pastry case in the preheated oven for 10 minutes.

Blanch the asparagus tips in boiling water for 2 minutes. Refresh in iced water, then drain.

Crack the eggs into a mixing bowl and whisk with the mustard and parsley until fully incorporated. Whisk in the milk and season.

Take the pastry case from the oven and remove the baking beans. Increase the oven temperature to 170°C/150°C Fan/Gas Mark 3½.

Lay the asparagus tips widthways across the tart case until the base is covered, then slowly pour over the egg mixture. Distribute the pieces of goat's cheese evenly on top of the tart. Cook in the oven for 25–35 minutes or until the egg mixture is set, then allow the tart to cool.

Pork and Apple Scotch Eggs

You need to taste these to understand why they are headliners in the picnic world and deserve to be given an encore time and time again. Great nestled in the hamper alongside the impressive Smoked Chicken, Apricot and Thyme Sausage Rolls (see page 135).

MAKES 4

7 eggs
1 large Bramley apple
25g butter
1 tablespoon chopped thyme
200g good-quality sausagemeat
200g minced pork
1 tablespoon chopped sage
1 tablespoon chopped parsley
1 tablespoon wholegrain mustard
50g plain flour
170g panko breadcrumbs
2 tablespoons dried sage
oil, for deep fat frying
sea salt and freshly ground black
    pepper

Place 4 eggs in a saucepan, cover with cold water and bring to the boil for 4 minutes, then remove and immediately refresh in ice-cold water. When eggs are completely cold, peel and pat dry, then leave to one side.

Peel and core the apple and cut into 5mm cubes. Add the butter to a frying pan and place over a medium heat. When the butter starts to froth, add the apple and thyme and cook for only 1 minute, shaking the pan until the apple starts to soften. Tip the apple onto kitchen paper and pat dry.

Place the sausagemeat, pork mince, chopped sage, parsley and mustard in a large bowl, season and mix well. Add the apple and thyme and mix gently, taking care not to break the apple.

Place a 30cm square of clingfilm on the table and lightly oil. Place a quarter of the sausagemeat mixture (around 125g) in the middle and spread it out, using your fingers, until it is large enough to encase the boiled egg.

Place the egg into the middle and, using the clingfilm, shape and mould the sausagemeat around the egg, making a smooth shape and ensuring the egg is sealed in. Wrap in the clingfilm. Repeat this process with the remaining 3 eggs and leave to chill in the fridge for 1 hour.

For the breadcrumb coating, crack the remaining 3 eggs into a bowl and beat. Place the flour in another bowl and season. Mix the panko breadcrumbs and dried sage in the third bowl. Remove the clingfilm from the chilled eggs, then roll first in the flour, then in the egg and lastly in the breadcrumbs; repeat this process again to ensure a good coating.

Heat the oil in a deep-fat fryer to 160°C. Place 1 egg in the deep-fat fryer at a time and cook for 6–7 minutes until crisp and golden. Repeat this process for the remaining eggs. Season and leave to cool, then serve.

Smoked Chicken, Apricot and Thyme Sausage Rolls

Holy moly, these are good! If these make it out your front door without a bite missing, we salute you! We sometimes serve this as one whole roll or cut and put in silicone paper bags with a wooden peg and gift tag.

SERVES 12–16

1 teaspoon olive oil
1 onion, chopped
2 garlic cloves, chopped
2 tablespoons chopped thyme,
    plus 1 teaspoon thyme leaves
300g minced pork
200g sausagemeat
150g smoked chicken breast, cut
    into 1cm dice
2 tablespoons chopped parsley
pinch of nutmeg
10 dried apricots, diced
50g breadcrumbs
flour, for dusting
150g shop-bought puff pastry
2 egg yolks, beaten
½ teaspoon rock salt
salt and freshly ground black
    pepper

Heat the olive oil in a frying pan, add the onion, garlic and chopped thyme and gently fry without colouring. Once the onions are soft, place the mixture into a bowl and leave to cool.

Place the minced pork, sausagemeat and smoked chicken in a large bowl. Add the parsley, nutmeg and apricots, then season with salt and pepper. Add the onion, garlic and thyme mixture to the bowl along with the breadcrumbs. Mix together to create the filling.

Dust a surface with flour and roll out the puff pastry to a rectangle 50 x 25cm, with a thickness of 1cm. Place the filling on the pastry and form it into a sausage shape down the length of the pastry, placing it off-centre. Brush the edges of the pastry with the beaten egg yolk. Fold the pastry over to create the sausage roll. Seal around the edges by pressing down with a fork. Using a sharp knife, slash the top of the sausage roll to create lines. Glaze with more of the beaten egg yolk, and sprinkle with the thyme leaves and rock salt. Rest in the fridge for 30 minutes.

Preheat the oven to 200°C/180°C Fan/Gas Mark 6.

Place the sausage roll in the preheated oven and bake for 10 minutes, then turn the oven down to 170°C/150°C Fan/Gas Mark 3½ and bake for a further 25–30 minutes until the pastry is golden.

Remove and place on a wire rack to cool. While still warm, cut into either small or large rolls.

Smash-it-up Picnic Eton Mess

This is a great one to get the kids involved – they can be the chief meringue smashers! Just make sure they leave a few meringue lumps in there…

MAKES 6

FOR THE MERINGUES
4 medium egg whites
240g caster sugar, plus extra for
    dusting

FOR THE ETON MESS
350ml double cream
20ml Marsala or brandy (optional)
2 tablespoons caster sugar
250g strawberries, halved and
    hulled
250g raspberries

Preheat the oven to 140°C/120°C Fan/Gas Mark 1. Line a baking tray with silicone or greaseproof paper and dust with a little caster sugar.

To make the meringues, whisk the egg whites in a food mixer until they stand up on their own in soft peaks. Continue whisking and slowly add half the sugar, making sure it is thoroughly incorporated into the egg whites. Remove the bowl from the mixer and very slowly fold in the remaining sugar by hand, using a large metal spoon. You should end up with a raw meringue that is thick and silky in texture and has a glossy sheen.

Using a large metal spoon, drop 4 big meringues onto the lined tray and cook them in the preheated oven for 1 hour, or until you can lift them off the tray. They need to be hard and crispy on the outside and lovely and chewy in the middle. When they are cooked, cool the meringues slowly.

Pour the cream, Marsala and caster sugar into a 550ml container with a tightly fitting lid. Take along with your strawberries, raspberries and homemade meringue on your picnic.

When ready to eat, shake your cream and Marsala mixture for 2 minutes to thicken it. Smash the meringue into pieces in individual bowls, add the strawberries and raspberries, then pour the cream over the top.

Chapter Eight:
Happy Holidays

This is where the inspiration for the book was born as every Christmas both Amber and I cook up lots of goodies, from chutneys and biscuits to glitter caramel. We then wrap them with the same love and attention as given to the cooking.

So happy holidays to you! Whatever holiday it is, bake, make and take around to special people in your life. It is also a perfect time and reason to give a gift from your heart to your neighbour, teacher or work colleagues and enjoy celebrating the holidays together.

Quirky fun food, from Pumpkin Pie Graveyards and scary Day of the Dead Red Velvet Skulls to an amazing fresh Challah Bread. One for sharing at work could be the Easter Bun Tear-and-share Tray for your coffee break.

Whatever the celebration throughout the year, enjoy the warmth and glow in your heart from giving.

Mini Egg Fairy Cakes

Who doesn't love mini eggs? It wouldn't be Easter without them!

MAKES 12

2 eggs
115g caster sugar
115g self-raising flour
115g unsalted butter, melted

TO DECORATE
510g icing sugar
330g unsalted butter
a few drops of natural food
   colouring, any colour
90g packet of mini eggs
edible glitter, for dusting

Preheat the oven to 180°C/160°C Fan/Gas Mark 4. Line a 12-hole cupcake tin with paper cases.

Whisk the eggs and sugar together until you have a light and fluffy mixture.

Combine the flour and butter together in a separate bowl, then gradually add the egg and sugar mixture to this, folding it in gently to make a smooth, stiff cake batter.

Carefully spoon the batter into the cupcake cases and bake in the preheated oven for 10–15 minutes until golden. Check to see if the cakes are ready by sticking a skewer into one – if it comes out clean the cakes are ready; if not, bake for another couple of minutes.

Remove the cakes from the oven and let them cool in the baking tray.

Whilst the cakes are cooling, make the icing. Whip the icing sugar and butter together until you get a pale fluffy buttercream, then add a few drops of food colouring, beating in the colour evenly. Spoon the buttercream into a piping bag. Pipe the buttercream on the top of each cake and decorate with mini eggs, then dust with edible glitter.

Easter Bun Tear-and-share Tray

You may have gathered we love the whole ethos of tear-and-share food. It gets people digging in and talking and this is what the holiday season is all about! Marzipan is much easier to grate if you freeze it first.

MAKES 10–12

250g strong flour
200g plain flour, plus extra for
    dusting
50g ground almonds
50g light soft brown sugar
200ml milk
7g active dried yeast
1 large egg, beaten
vegetable oil, for greasing

FOR THE FILLING
50g butter, melted
100g light soft brown sugar
2 tablespoons mixed spice
zest and juice of 1 lemon
25g mixed peel, chopped
75g currants
50g dried cranberries
75g marzipan, grated
6 tablespoons apricot jam

Line two 35 x 12cm baking tins with silicone paper, making sure you line the sides of the tin.

Sieve both flours into a large mixing bowl, add the ground almonds and sugar. Pour the milk into a saucepan and heat to 37°C, then whisk the yeast into the milk and remove from the heat. Make a well in the middle of the flour, pour the beaten egg and yeast milk into the well and mix together to form a dough.

Knead the dough on a floured work surface for 10–15 minutes, then place in a floured bowl, cover with oiled clingfilm and leave in a warm place to rise for 45 minutes or until doubled in size.

To make the filling, place the melted butter, sugar, mixed spice, lemon zest and juice in a bowl and mix thoroughly into a smooth paste. Fold in the mixed peel, currants, cranberries and grated marzipan.

Roll out the dough on a floured surface to a rectangle 40 x 30cm, 5mm thick. Spoon the filling onto the dough and spread out evenly, pressing it into the dough.

Roll the dough up tightly from one long side of the rectangle to form a sausage, then cut into 12 even rounds using a floured sharp knife.

Place 6 swirls in each lined tray, swirl side up, and flatten slightly with the palm of your hand, making sure to leave a small gap between each bun. Cover with oiled clingfilm and allow to rise for a further 45 minutes.

Preheat the oven to 170°C/150°C Fan/Gas Mark 3½.

Bake in the preheated oven for 30 minutes until golden brown, then allow to cool.

Melt the apricot jam with 2 tablespoons of water in a small pan over a gentle heat and brush evenly all over the buns for a glossy shine, then wrap to gift.

Marbled Chocolate Shards

Break the slab into shards and put into gift bags labelled with instructions to enjoy with a coffee to end the festive meal. You will be the talk of the table for your thoughtful gesture.

SERVES 6–8

200g dark chocolate
200g white chocolate
20g dried cranberries
20g dried apricots, chopped
20g pistachios, peeled and
    chopped

Melt the dark and white chocolate in separate heatproof bowls set over pans of simmering water until silky and smooth. Remove from the heat and allow to cool for 5–10 minutes.

Line a flat tray with silicone paper and pour on the melted dark chocolate, then the melted white chocolate. Carefully shake and tilt the tray until the chocolate has covered the base of the tray, then use a fork to swirl the chocolate into patterns.

Mix together the cranberries, apricots and pistachios, then sprinkle over the melted chocolate and allow to set in a cool place.

Once set, gently peel off the silicone paper, snap the chocolate into shards and bag.

Challah Bread

This is a beautiful egg-rich recipe and really hard to leave alone when it comes out the oven. It's screaming for our freshly made butter and homely chicken soup (see pages 39 and 164).

MAKES 1 LARGE LOAF OR 2 SMALL

2 x 7g packages of active dried yeast
100g plus 1 tablespoon caster sugar
120ml lukewarm water
5 extra-large egg yolks
3 extra-large eggs
3 tablespoons vegetable oil
1 tablespoon salt
650g strong plain flour, plus extra for dusting

FOR THE GLAZE
1 large egg
1 teaspoon vegetable oil
1 tablespoon sesame seeds

Dissolve the yeast and 1 tablespoon of sugar in the water in a small bowl. Let the mixture stand until it is foamy and has doubled in size.

Fit a mixer with the paddle blade. Beat the egg yolks and whole eggs in a large bowl with the mixer on high speed until light yellow in colour. Add the remaining sugar, the oil and salt and beat until blended. Reduce the speed to low and beat in the yeast mixture, then finally beat in the flour.

Knead the dough on a floured work surface for 5 minutes, then place in a generously buttered large bowl, turning the dough over once to coat it well with the butter. Cover the bowl with oiled clingfilm and leave to rise at room temperature for around 1 hour or until the dough has doubled in size.

Butter a baking sheet. Punch the dough down gently with your fist, then turn out onto a lightly floured surface. Cut the dough in to 3 equal pieces. Shape each piece into a rope about 40cm long and 4cm in diameter. Lay each rope side by side on the baking sheet. Starting from the middle, plait the ropes out to one end tucking the ends under. Turn the loaf and do the same with the other side, plaiting from the centre out and tucking the ends under.

Beat the egg with the vegetable oil, then brush the loaf with the egg glaze and sprinkle generously with sesame seeds. Cover with lightly oiled clingfilm and leave to rise for 30 minutes.

Preheat the oven to 180°C/160°C Fan/Gas Mark 4.

Bake the bread in the preheated oven for 30 minutes until golden and firm to the touch. Let the bread cool for 5 minutes on the baking sheet, then slide it onto a rack to cool for at least 10 minutes before slicing.

Pumpkin Pie Graveyards

Lots of fun for Halloween, this is a classic pumpkin purée with a modern twist of chocolate and ginger soil with its very own tombstones. Spooky!

MAKES 4

FOR THE PUMPKIN PIE
1 x 425g tin pumpkin purée
4 tablespoons caster sugar
1 teaspoon ground cinnamon
2 drops of vanilla extract
100ml double cream
2 ginger biscuits
2 Oreo biscuits

FOR THE TOMBSTONES
50g butter, cubed and softened
75g plain flour, sifted
25g caster sugar
2 drops of vanilla extract
40g chocolate, melted, for piping
sweetie bones or jelly snakes, to
    decorate

Place the pumpkin purée in a mixing bowl with the sugar, cinnamon and vanilla extract and stir together. In a separate bowl, whisk the cream until thick (do not over-whisk), then fold into the pumpkin purée. Spoon the pumpkin mixture into glasses, filling them three-quarters full, then refrigerate.

Place the ginger and Oreo biscuits in a blender and blitz into fine crumbs, then set aside.

To make the tombstones, rub the butter into the flour until it resembles fine breadcrumbs, then mix in the sugar and vanilla extract. Work the mixture until it forms a smooth ball and leaves the sides of the bowl clean. Cover the dough with clingfilm and refrigerate for 1 hour.

Preheat the oven to 140°C/120°C Fan/Gas Mark 1. Line a baking tray with baking parchment.

Remove the dough from the fridge and allow it to come up to room temperature. Lightly flour a work surface and roll the dough out until it is 1cm thick. Using tomb- and cross-shaped cutters, cut out the biscuits (you should be able to cut about 6 biscuits). Place on the lined baking tray and bake in the preheated oven for 30 minutes or until they are a very pale golden colour. Using a spatula or fish slice, carefully transfer to a wire rack.

To serve, spoon the ginger and Oreo crumbs on top of the purée. Pour the melted chocolate into a piping bag and pipe 'RIP' on each biscuit. Stick into the pumpkin mix and garnish with sweet bones.

Day of the Dead Red Velvet Skulls

A nod to Damien Hirst's stunning diamante skulls. These are glam and perfect for any 'day of the dead' or Halloween celebrations.

MAKES 8

180g butter, softened
300g golden caster sugar
1 teaspoon vanilla extract
3 large eggs
250ml buttermilk
375g self-raising flour
2 tablespoons cocoa powder
1 teaspoon bicarbonate of soda
1 tablespoon cider vinegar or
   white wine vinegar
2 tablespoons bright red food
   colour paste
edible glitter, to decorate

Preheat the oven to 170°C/150°C Fan/Gas Mark 3½.

Place the softened butter, sugar and vanilla extract in a mixing bowl and beat until light and fluffy. Slowly add the eggs, one at a time, beating between each, until you have a smooth batter. Add the buttermilk and beat together.

Sieve together the flour, cocoa powder and bicarbonate of soda, then fold into the batter until fully combined. Mix in the vinegar and red food colour paste.

Spoon into skull-shaped moulds and bake in the preheated oven for around 20 minutes. To test if the skulls are done, insert a skewer into the middle of the cake – if it comes out clean, it's cooked; if not, bake for another few minutes.

Pop the cakes from the moulds, place on a wire rack and dust with edible glitter.

Gingerbread Christmas Shapes

A fun present for little ones – bake and give with a little ready-made icing bag so they can decorate, keeping them entertained whilst the grown-ups are busy getting this festive show on the road!

MAKES 12–15

350g plain flour
1 teaspoon bicarbonate of soda
2 teaspoons ground ginger
1 teaspoon ground cinnamon
125g butter
175g light soft brown sugar
1 egg
4 tablespoons golden syrup
piping icing and cake decorations

Sift together the flour, bicarbonate of soda, ginger and cinnamon, then tip into the bowl of a food processor. Add the butter and blend until you have a breadcrumb-like texture. Stir in the sugar.

In another bowl, beat the egg and golden syrup together. Add to the flour mixture and pulse until you have a dough. Tip the dough out onto the work surface and knead briefly until smooth. Wrap in clingfilm and leave to chill in the fridge for 15 minutes.

Preheat the oven to 180°C/160°C Fan/Gas Mark 4 and line 2 baking trays with greaseproof paper.

Roll the dough out to a thickness of 5mm on a lightly floured surface. Use Christmas-shaped cutters to cut out shapes and place on the baking trays, leaving large gaps between them as they expand during baking.

Bake for 12–15 minutes until golden brown. Leave on the tray for 10 minutes, then transfer to a wire rack to finish cooling. When cool, decorate with piping icing and cake decorations.

Festive Wreath Crunchies

We love a bit of glitter and these festive wreaths will provide some seasonal glitz. Prepare to get messy and gooey, and work quickly before the mix sets. This idea goes perfectly with the Gingerbread Christmas Shapes as you can tie red ribbon on both and hang them on the Christmas tree – the perfect edible gift for friends and family.

MAKES 12–15

75g unsalted butter, at room
    temperature
200g mini marshmallows
2 tablespoons golden syrup
1 teaspoon green gel colouring
150g cornflakes
50g rice krispies
30g pistachios, chopped
50g red jelly beans, cut in half
    widthways
1 teaspoon edible green glitter

Line a baking tray with silicone or baking parchment.

Place the butter, marshmallows and golden syrup in a large heatproof bowl set over a pan of boiling water and stir continuously until they have melted together. Remove the bowl from the heat and stir in the green food colouring. Add the cornflakes, rice krispies and pistachios and gently fold together.

Spoon the mixture onto the lined tray to create small mounds (about 1 tablespoon of mixture per mound). Before the mixture sets, warm your hands under hot water then create a hole in the middle of each mound to form a wreath. Dot with the red jellybeans to create 'berries' and sprinkle with edible glitter.

Once cool, box and present.

Santa's Coal

Edible fun for all those naughty boys and girls!

MAKES 25–30

450g Oreo biscuits
60g currants
60g butter
300g marshmallows
edible black lustre dust, for
    dusting

Line a 25 x 15 x 3cm baking tin with baking parchment.

Place the Oreos and currants in a blender and blitz into fine crumbs, then pour into a large mixing bowl.

Place the butter and marshmallows together in a heatproof bowl set over a pan of boiling water and allow to melt. Once melted, pour into the Oreo crumbs and mix together with warm wet hands to bind. Tip the mixture into the lined tray, packing it in firmly, then smooth the top. Allow to set for 1 hour.

Cut into coal-shaped lumps and dust with edible lustre dust.

Homemade Christmas Spirit Mincemeat

A really thoughtful gift for those who love to make their own mince pies. Presented in a beautiful preserving jar, this will set the season off to good cheer (but remember to make in advance as it needs time to mature).

MAKES A 1.5 LITRE JAR

150g sultanas
150g golden raisins
150g currants
150g dried cranberries
150g golden berries (optional)
300ml brandy or rum
200ml sherry
zest and juice of 1 orange
zest and juice of 1 lemon
200g shredded vegetable suet
250g dark brown sugar
75g chopped mixed peel
½ nutmeg, grated
1 Bramley apple, peeled and grated
1 pear, peeled and grated

Soak the sultanas, raisins, currants, dried cranberries and golden berries, if using, in a bowl with the brandy and sherry for 4–6 hours until plump and swollen.

Drain the fruit, reserving the brandy and sherry to one side. Mix all the other ingredients into the soaked fruit, then finally add the brandy and sherry and gently stir to combine.

Spoon into a sterilised jar, seal and store in a cool, dark room to mature for up to 6 months.

Chapter Nine:
Heavenly Hampers

Heavenly hampers are a bespoke fun gift collaboration to give and share the love in any situation, with most to be cooked, wrapped and eaten on the day.

Here are five of our favourite goody boxes! Beginning with the Off to Uni Kit for the time when friends or offspring are off to college, this hamper will see them through the boozy fresher's week with the comfort of the home-cooked carb-loaded Penne and Mushroom Preserving Jar and Garlic Dough Balls. The next time you get an invite to a barbecue, instead of just turning up with beer and a bottle of wine, take the BBQ Box with rubs, sauces and the best kimchi ever! If visiting unwell friends, prepare the Get Well Soon Hamper, ideal with a cup of tea and time spent together. Amber thought up the Heartbreak Hamper for a girls' night in, packed with some real classics. See in the happy holidays with our selection, which includes the perfect Turkey Butter and Seasoning Kit, Rich Bread Sauce and Sparkling Star Cranberry Sauce.

Off to Uni Kit

All full of carbs and the comfort of home cooking – ideal before a night out – plus an early livener for the morning after!

Penne and Mushroom Preserving Jar

SERVES 4

400g dried penne pasta
4 tablespoons olive oil
1 leek, sliced into 1cm rounds
1 large onion, finely chopped
3 cloves garlic, crushed
300g mixed mushrooms, sliced
200ml white wine (optional)
1 vegetable stock cube
1 tablespoon wholegrain mustard
568ml double cream
½ bunch of basil leaves, torn
50g Parmesan cheese, grated
sea salt and freshly ground black pepper

Fill a large saucepan with salted water and bring to the boil. Add the pasta and stir, then bring to a rolling boil for 11–13 minutes until tender and cooked al dente. Remove, place in a colander and refresh under cold running water. Drain the pasta thoroughly, then pat dry with kitchen paper.

Place a large saucepan over a medium heat, add 2 tablespoons of the oil and heat, then add the leek, onion and garlic and cook without colouring for about 5 minutes. Turn up the heat, then add another tablespoon of olive oil, add the mushrooms and fry for 8–10 minutes, until cooked through.

Add the white wine (or water if you prefer), stock cube (making sure it dissolves) and mustard to the pan, then stir thoroughly into the mushrooms and onions. Reduce for 3–5 minutes, stirring continually to ensure it doesn't stick.

Pour in the double cream, bring to the boil and cook for 8–10 minutes until reduced by a third, stirring occasionally. Gently tip in the cooked pasta, season and stir together for a further 2 minutes, making sure it's hot for serving.

Place in a large preserving jar, add the torn basil leaves, Parmesan and the final tablespoon of olive oil. Serve with freshly ground black pepper.

ON THE LABEL, WRITE:
Heat me and eat me.

Hair of the Dog

SERVES 4

2 teaspoons celery salt
4 leafy middles of the celery stalk
1 tablespoon Worcestershire sauce
1 litre tomato juice
4 small Tabasco minatures, or 1 small bottle
4 x 50ml good-quality vodka miniatures

Tip the celery salt onto a small plate. Wet the rim of 4 glasses and dip in the celery salt. Place a leafy stem of celery for stirring inside each glass.

Add the Worcestershire sauce to the tomato juice then package with the small bottles of Tabasco sauce and the vodka miniatures.

Garlic Dough Balls

SERVES 4

15g fresh yeast or 7g packet active dried yeast
140ml warm water
250g strong white flour, sieved, plus extra for
    dusting
½ teaspoon caster sugar
pinch of sea salt
2 garlic cloves, finely chopped
2 tablespoons finely chopped chives

FOR THE GARLIC BUTTER
125g butter, softened
1 teaspoon sea salt
2 tablespoons chopped parsley
3 garlic cloves, finely chopped
¼ teaspoon smoked paprika

In a large mixing bowl, stir the yeast into the warm water. Stir until it has fully dissolved, then use your hands to mix in the flour, sugar, salt, garlic and chives until it forms a dough that easily comes away from the sides of the bowl. If the mix is a little dry and crumbly, add a splash of warm water.

Flour a work surface and firmly knead the dough for about 10 minutes until it is nice and elastic. Place in a lightly floured bowl or tray, loosely cover with lightly oiled clingfilm and leave in a warm place to rise until it has doubled in size (an airing cupboard for 30 minutes is perfect!).

Briefly re-knead the dough on a floured work surface and form into a ball. Cut the ball into quarters, and then divide each piece into 4 so you end up with 16 pieces.

Lightly dust the work surface again with flour and firmly roll each piece to a walnut-sized ball. Line a large baking tray with baking parchment paper, then place on the dough balls, leaving enough space for them to prove and double in size. Cover again with lightly oiled clingfilm and leave in a warm place for 30–40 minutes.

Preheat the oven to 180°C/160°C Fan/Gas Mark 4. When the dough balls have proved, bake in the preheated oven for 15 minutes until they are a pale golden brown. Allow to cook, then cool.

To make the garlic butter, place the softened butter in a bowl and add the salt, parsley and finally the garlic and paprika, then beat with a wooden spoon until all ingredients are thoroughly mixed together. Pack into a lidded container.

LABEL WITH THE FOLLOWING:
Reheat the dough balls in the oven at 180°C/160°C Fan/Gas Mark 4 for 3–5 minutes and serve with the garlic butter.

Get Well Soon Hamper

Super-fresh vitamin-bursting juice and a real homely hot chicken soup given in a flask,
plus a beautiful old-fashioned tea loaf and a cup of tea, shared with an elderly loved one
who may just want a little of your time and attention.

Chicken Soul Food Soup

SERVES 10 (CAN BE FROZEN)

1 onion, finely chopped
4 garlic cloves, finely chopped
1 large leek, sliced into 1cm rounds
4 large carrots, sliced into 1cm rounds
2 celery sticks, sliced into 1cm rounds
2 tablespoons vegetable oil
1 tablespoon wholegrain mustard
1 chicken (about 1kg)
2–3 litres good-quality chicken stock
3 sprigs of thyme
2 bay leaves
6 Savoy cabbage leaves, finely shredded
80g frozen peas
salt and freshly ground black pepper

Place the onion, garlic, leek, carrots and celery
in a large saucepan, making sure the pan can
accommodate the whole chicken. Add the oil and
mustard, stir together and place on a medium heat
for 10 minutes.

Gently place the chicken on top of the vegetables,
season with a little salt and plenty of black pepper,
then pour the stock around the chicken, making
sure it is completely covered. Add the thyme and
bay leaves. Cover with a lid, turn up the heat and
bring up to a rapid boil.

Once boiling, turn down to a rolling simmer and
leave to cook for 40 minutes. Remove from the heat,
remove the lid and allow the chicken to cool in the
stock for around 30 minutes.

Carefully take out the whole chicken. Pick the
meat from the carcass and roughly chop into small
pieces.

Place the pan of stock over a high heat and bring
back to a rapid boil, leaving the lid off. Boil for
about 20 minutes until the liquid has reduced by
about one third.

Remove the bay leaves and thyme from the pan and
discard. Add the shredded cabbage to the stock with
the peas, then add the chopped chicken and bring
back to the boil. Season and pour into a flask. Any
additional soup can be stored in the fridge for up to
2 days or frozen.

Malted Earl Grey and Prune Tea Loaf

MAKES 1 LOAF

8 tablespoons malt extract
1 tablespoon black treacle
100ml hot strong Earl Grey or English Breakfast Tea
  (use 2 tea bags)
200g pitted prunes, quartered
butter, for greasing
175g self-raising flour
1 teaspoon ground mixed spice
1 egg

Mix the malt extract and treacle into the hot tea and stir until dissolved. Place the prunes in a mixing bowl, pour over the hot malt tea mixture and leave to cool.

Preheat the oven to 140°C/120°C Fan/Gas Mark 1. Butter a 900g loaf tin and line with baking parchment.

Sift the flour and mixed spice into a large mixing bowl, add the egg and tea mixture and stir to combine well. Spoon into the lined loaf tin and bake in the preheated oven for 1–1¼ hours. Test the loaf is done by piercing with a skewer – when the skewer comes out clean the loaf is ready; if not, bake for another few minutes.

Leave the loaf to stand for 10 minutes in the tin, then turn out onto a wire rack. Once cool, wrap the loaf in baking parchment and place in an airtight container for a minimum of 2 days to mature. This loaf gets better with time.

Green Goddess Vitamin Juice

MAKES 1 LARGE BOTTLE

3 pineapple chunks
200ml apple juice
⅓ apple
1 large broccoli floret
1 small handful spinach
1 celery stick
1½ teaspoons linseeds
20g fresh ginger
2.5cm piece cucumber
1 small handful of watercress
3 stems parsley
⅓ avocado
6 ice cubes

Blitz all the ingredients in a blender until smooth, then pour into a sterilised bottle and seal. To be drunk as soon as possible while all the nutrients are at their best.

BBQ Box

Summer is officially here and the bbq invites are coming in thick and fast! As much as it's nice to receive a crate of beer or bottle of vino, why not set yourself aside some time to come up with something a little more thoughtful.

Kimchi

MAKES 1 LARGE JAR

800g Chinese cabbage
6 tablespoons sea salt
1.5 litre bottle distilled water
25g fresh ginger, grated
6 garlic cloves, crushed
1 teaspoon caster sugar
3 tablespoons fish sauce
3 tablespoons Korean red chilli flakes
250g large carrots, cut into matchsticks
250g white radish, cut into matchsticks
6 spring onions, cut into 2.5cm pieces

Cut the cabbage in half lengthways, then into quarters. Remove the core and slice the cabbage into 5cm strips. Place the cabbage in a large bowl, add the salt and mix with your hands for about 2 minutes until the cabbage starts to soften.

Add the water to cover the cabbage – the cabbage needs to be submerged in the water so use a dinner plate to weigh it down if necessary. Leave for 3 hours, stirring occasionally.

Drain the cabbage and rinse under cold running water for about 3 minutes, then leave to drain in a colander for 20–30 minutes.

Place the ginger, garlic, sugar and fish sauce in a bowl and mix to make a paste, then fold in the chilli flakes.

Gently squeeze any remaining water from the cabbage, place in a large mixing bowl with the carrots, white radish and spring onions. Spoon in the paste. Wearing gloves, gently massage the paste into the cabbage and vegetable mix until thoroughly coated.

Pack the kimchi into a sterilised preserving jar, pushing it down so it is tightly packed. Allow the juice to rise and cover the vegetables, then seal the jar. Let the jar sit in a cool dark place for 24–48 hours – place the jar on a plate as the kimchi will bubble and ferment and may leak out of the jar.

After a maximum of 48 hours, open the jar and push the kimchi down (this will release any air), then reseal. This will last in the fridge for 4 weeks.

Bourbon Sticky Rib Sauce

MAKES 700ML

400ml tomato ketchup
6 tablespoons maple syrup
125ml bourbon whiskey
2 tablespoons muscovado sugar
1 tablespoon Worcestershire sauce
1 tablespoon white wine vinegar
2 red chillies, deseeded and finely chopped
zest and juice of 2 limes
100ml cola
1 tablespoon smoked salt
1 tablespoon smoked paprika
1 tablespoon garlic salt

Place all the ingredients in a large mixing bowl and whisk together, then pour into sterilised bottles.

Super Rub

MAKES 75G

1 tablespoon each of garlic salt, cumin, English mustard powder, zahter, smoked salt or rock salt, smoked paprika, chopped dried chillies

Place all the ingredients in a bag and shake until thoroughly mixed together. Pour into a jar and label.

Heartbreak Hamper

Oh girls … cue the Gloria Gaynor 'I will survive' track and put that waste of space behind you! If your bestie is going through a little heartbreak, help her over that hill and show her the new horizon of possibilities.

'Plenty More Fish in the Sea' Mini Lobster Brioche Rolls

MAKES 8

250g cooked lobster meat, chopped
5 tablespoons mayonnaise
¼ teaspoon wasabi
1 teaspoon chopped tarragon
juice of 1 lime
8 mini brioche rolls
sea salt and freshly ground black pepper

Place the chopped lobster meat in a bowl, fold in the mayonnaise, wasabi and tarragon, then squeeze in the lime juice and season.

Split the brioche rolls down the middle and fill with the lobster mixture, package and place in your hamper.

'Good Riddance' Champagne and Pink Rhubarb Bellini

SERVES 4

250g rhubarb
50g caster sugar
½ teaspoon vanilla extract
200ml water
1 bottle Champagne

Peel and chop the rhubarb into 5mm rounds and place in a heavy-based saucepan. Add the sugar,

vanilla extract and water. Gently bring to the boil over a medium heat for 2 minutes, then turn the heat down and gently simmer for a further 5–10 minutes until soft and tender.

Pour into a sterilised jar. Place in the hamper with Champagne and a spoon.

ON THE LABEL WRITE:
Spoon into Champagne glasses and top up with fizz when it's time to party.

'Dry Your Eyes Princess' Cucumber Soother

MAKES 300ML

¾ green apple
5cm cucumber piece
6 stems parsley
1 handful spinach
½ avocado
1½ teaspoons lemon juice
1½ teaspoons linseeds
200ml fresh apple juice
6 ice cubes

Blitz all the ingredients in a blender until smooth, pour into a sterilised bottle and pop in the hamper.

It Was Always a 'Rocky Road'

MAKES 6–8 BARS

100g unsalted butter, softened
150g dark chocolate (preferably 72% cocoa solids)
150g Mars Bars, chopped
3 tablespoons golden syrup
250g plain digestive biscuits
100g dried cranberries
100g mini marshmallows
60g hazelnuts, chopped

Line a 25 x 15 x 4cm cake tin with clingfilm.

Melt the butter, chocolate, Mars Bars and golden syrup together in a heatproof bowl placed over a saucepan of boiling water. Once everything has

melted, give the mixture a stir to blend it properly, then take it off the heat and allow to cool slightly.

Put the biscuits in a sealable plastic food bag and smash them up using a rolling pin. Add the cranberries, marshmallows and hazelnuts to the bag of biscuit crumbs, give it good shake to mix, then tip out into the bowl of melted chocolate.

Thoroughly mix all the ingredients and tip the chocolate mixture into the lined tin, making sure you spread it evenly. Place in the fridge for about 2 hours until it has set.

Once the mixture is solid, pop the cake out of the tin, using the clingfilm as leverage, cut it into bars and wrap for the hamper.

Happy Holidays Hamper

When we make our hampers for the holiday season, this is always a must. People really seem to appreciate the turkey rub and butter hand-tied in silicone paper and twisted into a cracker, while jars of homemade bread sauce and sparkling cranberry sauce make a really thoughtful, seasonal gift.

Rich Bread Sauce

MAKES 1 SMALL JAR

1 onion, peeled
4 whole cloves
4 bay leaves
300ml milk
250ml double cream
200g soft white breadcrumbs
30g butter
fresh nutmeg
salt and freshly ground black pepper

Stud the onion with the cloves and the bay leaves (if necessary, make a small slit in the outer layer of the onion with a knife). Place in a saucepan, add the milk and cream, then slowly heat the milk and gently poach the onion for about 20 minutes.

Lift the onion out of the pan and carefully remove the cloves and bay leaves. Pour the milk into a blender, add the onion and blitz together, gradually adding the breadcrumbs until you have the correct consistency – it should be similar to a loose porridge.

Finally add the butter and stir. Season with salt and black pepper, then grate some nutmeg on to taste. Pack into a sterilised jar and keep in the fridge until ready to use.

Turkey Butter and Seasoning Kit

MAKES 1 TUBE

FOR THE TURKEY BUTTER
250g butter, at room temperature
1 tablespoon white wine vinegar
1 tablespoon grainy mustard
1 tablespoon lemon juice
1 tablespoon smoked salt
1 tablespoon smoked paprika
1 tablespoon garlic powder
1 tablespoon cracked black pepper
¼ bunch tarragon or parsley, chopped

FOR THE SEASONING KIT
3 tablespoons rock salt
1 teaspoon cracked black pepper
2 teaspoons garlic salt
2 teaspoons dried thyme
2 teaspoons dried rosemary
1 teaspoon dried sage
1 teaspoon English mustard powder
1 teaspoon garlic powder

Place the butter in a mixing bowl and gently stir in all the other ingredients, ensuring they are thoroughly mixed together. Spoon the butter in a line along the edge of a sheet of baking parchment, roll the paper into a tube, then twist each end to make a cracker. Store in the fridge for up to 1 month.

For the seasoning kit, thoroughly mix all ingredients, spoon into a bag and label.

Sparkling Star Cranberry Sauce

MAKES 500ML

600ml cranberry juice
450g cranberries
150g muscovado sugar
50ml Cointreau
zest and juice of 1 orange
2 teaspoons edible glitter

Place the cranberry juice in a large heavy-based saucepan and bring to the boil, then simmer for about 10 minutes until reduced by half.

Add the cranberries, sugar and Cointreau and bring to the boil. Turn down the heat and simmer for 10–15 minutes, then add the orange zest and juice. Sprinkle in the edible glitter, stir and pour into sterilised jars. Seal while the mixture is still hot.

Index

Acknowledgements

A book like this involves a journey and many people.

I would firstly like to thank Emma Shutler who has not only been a major help on this book but also on the two previous books. Emma is all the things I'm not – disciplined, detailed and organised. Thank you, Emma, for putting *Delicious Gifts* into some sort of sense and shape before it was sent to our lovely editor, Gillian Haslam, who has a real understanding of cookery writing – a true quality editor.

Karen Thomas is an amazing cake maker and decorator in her own right. Foolishly, after lots of wine at our local pub, The Pier, she said she wanted to help and get amongst the recipe trialling. Karen gave up countless weekends in weighing, cooking and amending recipes alongside myself. She's been a great support throughout and very patient!

Chef Murray Tapiki and Stephanie Lykourgou for supporting me through all the beauty shots within this book. Also The Club at the Cafe Royale, London, for giving me a quiet and creative space whilst writing and bringing it all together – thank you one and all.

Photographer Jodi Hinds understood totally what I wanted from this book. Jodi has a wonderful smile and a lovely heart – a real fun person with a serious creative eye in food photography. It was a joy from the first time we met, leading on to a mad week of food photography with challenging deadlines to create this picture-friendly book.

Enter Katie Cecil, personal friend to Amber and I who totally gets what we're about. Katie is an amazing stylist with a natural-born gift for making all things look beautiful. Katie makes it all look very easy; she is driven, passionate and really cares. She is a true perfectionist and a lovely friend.

Thank you to the Bloomsbury team and Absolute Press – to Jon Croft and Meg Avent for having the confidence in book three, to Kim Musgrove for art direction and to Emily North for keeping it all on track, for being forgiving on deadlines and being a point of contact and support to me – you're a shining star.

Lastly, my adorable, beautiful wife Amber inspired and has been part of this book with her amazing creative touch. Thank you Amber for sharing and putting up with another book invading and taking over the last year of our lives! You're my rock, inspiration and best friend. Thank you x

Made with Love x

Publisher Jon Croft
Commissioning Editor Meg Avent
Art Direction Kim Musgrove and Matt Inwood
Designers Kim Musgrove and Allison Curtis
Project Editor Emily North
Recipe Editor Gillian Haslam
Photographer Jodi Hinds
Food Stylist Katie Cecil
Proofreader Margaret Haynes
Indexer Zoe Ross